# color + design
## transforming interior space

**Ron Reed**

**University of North Texas**

**MS, NCIDQ, ASID, IDEC, IIDA**

**FAIRCHILD BOOKS**
**NEW YORK**

Executive Editor: Olga T. Kontzias

Senior Associate Acquisitions Editor: Jaclyn Bergeron

Assistant Acquisitions Editor: Amanda Breccia

Editorial Development Director: Jennifer N. Crane

Development Editor: Michelle Levy

Associate Art Director: Erin Fitzsimmons

Production Director: Ginger Hillman

Senior Production Editor: Elizabeth Marotta

Photo Researcher: Avital Aronowitz

Copyeditor: Joanne Slike

Cover Design: Erin Fitzsimmons

Cover Art: front cover © Pieter Estersohn/Beateworks/Corbis; back cover © Kenneth Johansson/
Corbis (left), Veer (center), and © Pieter Estersohn/Beateworks/Corbis (right)

Text Design: Barbara Barg Medley

Library of Congress Catalog Card Number: 2009925255

ISBN: 978-1-56367-602-4

GST R 133004424

Printed in China

TP11

# contents

# extended contents

**FIGURE P.1** Colorful landscape at Teton National Park, Wyoming. (© Morey Milbradt/Brand X/Corbis)

# preface

This book is about color—not color science or color art, but rather a design process for using color confidently: a visual training tool for seeing the spatial transformations that occur with successful and not-so-successful color applications. As an educator who teaches color, I have found over the years many wonderful resources on the topic, but few have been available that focus specifically on the visual aspect of the process where color is realized in an interior. The book is organized to present color theory side by side with the principles of design.

At the root of all design are the principles and elements of design. The principles and elements, like wood and nails, help to create a building. And a building, like color, needs a foundation to keep if from falling apart. Just as interior space is influenced by the building, color is influenced by its surroundings. A designer cannot use color independently without taking other variables into consideration that can significantly impact its use. Interior spaces are created with all or part of the principles and elements of design and variations of their applications. The elements of design consist of color, space, line, form, shape, texture, and pattern. The principles of design consist of balance (radial, symmetrical, asymmetrical), rhythm (repetition of size, shape, or color), emphasis, proportion, scale, unity, harmony, and variety (see Table P.1). The process whereby designers decide how the color is to be used in conjunction with the principles of design, discussed in this book as the *color design process,* is intended to make your use of color more successful. Color helps users connect to the space more than any other design element. This connection should satisfy the personal needs, both physical and psychological, of the user of interior space without compromising the integrity of the design. Poor color usage can destroy even the best design intentions. The process of designing follows a set of guiding laws or principles for examining the

success of new concepts and ideas. By following the color design process, you will find your own palettes to explore and use. Absent the strong pull of color trends, any imaginable color can be used without a preconceived notion of what is and is not appropriate.

Beginning design students are introduced to a core of design values referred to as the elements and principles. These two categories hold the basic concepts for communication within all design professions and are the tools for creativity and execution of design ideas. Color in conjunction with the design principles can be used to help organize interior space. The principles of design are the core of any successful design project. Whether you're a novice designer or an experienced professional, understanding how to use the principles of design well is critical. These are our tools for achieving any successful design solution, for aesthetics, or to protect the health, safety, and welfare of our clients.

Pentti Routio (2004) identifies specific goals that all design should acquire: usability—utility and function; beauty—aesthetics (principles and elements of design); meaning—messages sent; ecology—impact on the environment; economy—value and price; and safety. Our relationship to art, architecture, and interior design is a personal one based on the way we perceive our surroundings and our natural environment via our senses. Beginning design students must understand how to use the elements of design (color, in this case) in coordination with the principles of design for the outcomes to be effective, appropriate, and creative.

Just as we use color to code and organize our office files, color can be applied with the principle of balance to bring order to our surroundings and communicate the identity of the space. Color provides an additional stimulus to help

**TABLE P.1.** Principles and Elements of Design

| PRINCIPLE | DEFINITION |
|---|---|
| Balance | Refers to the relationship of colored elements as they occupy an applied axis within a space perceived to be equal in visual weight. |
| | **Symmetrical** (Formal balance) Elements on either side of an implied axis are equally balanced and of the same shape and form (*mirror image*). |
| | **Asymmetrical** (Informal balance) Elements on either side of an implied axis are equal weight but vary in shape and size. Often more visually interesting and can be achieved through value and/or hue contrast. |
| | **Radial** Balance achieved by the equal rotation of design elements around a central axis. |
| Rhythm | Movement or path created by related visual elements, resulting in a constant pattern. |
| | **Repetition** A continued, even sequence of the same design element within a space. |
| | **Alternation** The alternation between two different design elements by pattern, shape, or color where the eye follows in a rhythmic motion. |
| | **Progression** The progression of design element from large to small or small to large. |
| Emphasis | Also called focal point, indicates attention drawn between colored elements within a space through one of the seven types of color contrast. |
| Proportion | Refers to the relationship of the individual parts of a composition to the whole. |
| Scale | Represents the actual size of an object relative to its surroundings. |
| Unity | Opposite of variety, focuses on the whole rather than the individual parts within a composition or space, using colors that create a balanced relationship |
| Harmony | The agreement or compatibility of colored components in a composition or space. |
| Variety | The continual change and variation of design elements (shape, size, color, and texture) through subtle changes in contrast. |

| ELEMENT | DEFINITION |
|---|---|
| Color | The natural quality of an object that when reflected by light produces the visible spectrum. |
| Space | The combination of the elements and principles of design used to create a three-dimensional inhabitable environment. |
| Line | The connection between two points (vertical, horizontal, curved, diagonal, or free-form). |
| Form | Three-dimensional mass of shapes. |
| Shape | Two-dimensional shapes including square, rectangle, circle, and triangle. |
| Texture | The perceptual or physical qualities of material that result in a visual and/or tactile experience such as rough or smooth. |
| Pattern | The repetition of shapes and forms. |

us decipher and decode the overwhelming amount of visual information we encounter on a daily basis. Too much color can oversaturate our visual field, and too much of the same color can create monotony, too much blending, and the loss of important visual cues within our environment.

The principles and elements of design have often been referred to by designers as the basic theory and concepts for describing and creating interior space. Their importance should be considered as integral to understanding the complexity of color. Funneling design properties with color facilitates an approachable and accessible method for working through complexity to confidently use color in personal and professional applications.

The color design process presented in this book refers to the way designers use the principles of design to solve color design problems. Combining design principles with smart use of color is necessary to realize a final design that has quality, long-lasting functional value, and aesthetic appeal. The principles should not be regarded as definite rules in the design process, but rather as tools that can help the process.

Beginning design students are anxious to work with color and choose color for fabrics, finishes, and building materials. Interior design is a visual profession. Students of any design discipline are visual learners. The more visual aids available, the more we increase a student's awareness of the process and application of color. Applying color in any space is part science, part intuition, and part luck. We have learned through trial and error that choosing and applying color is more complicated than it seems. Color must be carefully understood to ensure it is used well; however, many new designers learn on the job, making critical mistakes in order to learn what works and what doesn't work. Color is crucial to the overall quality of the finished design.

Now, where to begin? A common dilemma experienced when searching through trade publications, books, and magazines is the wide range of interior photos available. In many respects, these photos may not illustrate a significant use of color, relying instead on schemes composed of neutral palettes occasionally accented with color. This void leaves a lack of access to good visuals in teaching color palettes for interior design. Second, what if we could go back in time and change these interiors, to "reassign" the color palette? In addition to positive changes in color within a space, demonstrations of poor color usage could help students see both successful and unsuccessful approaches to using color. This is an invaluable visual tool for design students to see how to avoid making color errors. Design students are rarely able to see the full color transformations that can take place by including all design elements (finishes/materials) that compose our living environments.

This book will assist the reader with photos of projects that illustrate how a space takes on different spatial characters through color manipulation. Each example will show alternative color solutions, with a picture illustrating improper use of color. Each section will provide a series of study problems to be used in the instruction of color. Each study problem will include the study purpose, the design process, learning objectives, intended outcomes, and supplies needed for execution where applicable.

Chapter 1 is an introduction to basic color theory and systems for color management commonly used within the design industry. Properties of light and color, physiological processes of color vision, and color systems are discussed. It is very difficult to systemize or create a "magic formula" for using color. The complexity of color has been studied by many theorists. This chapter presents the works of Newton, Munsell, Albers, Itten, and Birren.

Chapter 2 examines the psychological responses to color, color associations, and perceptions that shape the way we interact with color in the built environment. Imagine for one moment a world without color, a black and white land void of blue skies and green grasslands. As a communication tool, color is imperative to our daily activities. We use color to convey messages to each other, whether it is a red light that signals a driver to stop, a yellow and black sign that warns of potential danger, or a bouquet of red roses that expresses our love. With the relatively recent terrorist attacks in the United States, the government introduced a five-color warning system to inform the public of potential terrorist threats, with green as the lowest level and red as the highest. Color has the power to change our

feelings, to express our personalities, to convey excitement, a sense of professionalism, or melancholy. Color is a personal choice that reflects who we are, sharing information about ourselves with those with whom we come into contact.

Chapter 3 introduces the first principle of design: balance. Balance typically refers to a balance of proportion, though color balance also affects the interior. It discusses the four types of balance achieved with color: value contrast (light/dark), hue balance (complements), intensity contrast (bright/dull), and size of color area (large/small). This chapter also presents methods to visually manipulate perceived spatial size by balancing the volume of the interior with color.

Chapter 4 deals with color and rhythm. Five types of rhythm are discussed in this chapter: repetition, alternation, progression, continuation, and radiation. This chapter examines natural forms as inspiration for natural color rhythm.

Chapter 5 examines color and emphasis and how contrast is critical for effective points of visual interest. Color is one of the first elements that attracts attention and begins the initial experience of a place. This chapter presents contrast of hue and value, contrast of design feature (shape and form), contrast of texture, emphasis with color dominance, and contrast of anomaly to generate points of interest within the interior.

Chapter 6 discusses color proportion and scale by introducing practical applications of color to change perception of spatial size. This chapter is a preface to Chapter 7, which is concerned with establishing harmonious spatial proportions with color.

Chapter 7 presents the seven color harmonies commonly used for interior color palettes: monochromatic, complementary, split complementary and double complementary, analogous, triadic and tetrad, multi-hue, and achromatic. Illustrations of each harmony will be presented and discussed, along with interior examples to reinforce the harmonic color concepts.

Chapter 8 examines color and variety as key principles to stimulate our visual experiences. This chapter discusses color and the elements of line, shape, pattern, and texture to add interest and excitement to enhance and modify the interior space.

In Chapter 9 on color and culture, we peer into five cultures across the globe and compare the differences in color meanings, symbolism, and social customs that shape each culture's perceptions of colors. In doing so, we also generate a deeper appreciation of our differences.

This research, ever important to understanding the presence of color in our lives, yields practical methods for working quickly and efficiently. Color should be studied holistically, as a part of the larger contexts of design, and within the totality of design theory. Exploring the various faces of color as they relate to the principles of design, balance, rhythm, emphasis, proportion and scale, harmony and unity, and variety provides an enriched way of learning about color and design.

A designer might find balance and rhythm to be the key factors in the creation of a room and proportion and emphasis to be less prominent in the final design. Depending on your goal, these tools can be used at your discretion. The point to be made is they cannot be ignored altogether. They are essential to the arguable terms "good design" or "bad design." Design is a personal experience for each individual. What one person finds ugly, a second person may find beautiful. Elevating design beyond everyday experiences can be achieved by understanding the principles of design well and utilizing them creatively and logically to execute a vision, concept, or idea.

Anyone wishing to study color must work independently to discover the nuances of color. The skill of an interior designer is what clients rely on when they choose colors that support a healthy, stimulating, and comfortable environment to live or work in. However, the majority of people have either never worked with a designer or attempted to make color choices for themselves without the aid of designer or color consultant. More and more, paint companies are making it easier for the general public to learn about color with educational tools and interactive software available on the Web, preselected color palettes within their lines, and publications on color basics. Appendix B provides a list of interactive color Web sites to hone your color skills. Intuition and a sense of "good taste" tend to drive more color design decisions than a prescriptive, scientific method of choosing the right palette. In this text, we seek new ways to simplify the color evaluation process and make it more enjoyable.

Predetermined color palettes available in retail store are necessary in some cases for those wary to begin color selection on their own. For the consumer, paint manufacturers have done an excellent job of eliminating the sometimes torturous task of deciding what color to use and then choosing two to three other hues that work well with the color. However, predetermined color palettes do not aid the novice designer in knowing *where* the color placement and distribution should be within the space and to what interior elements the colors should be assigned. Without some knowledge of where and how to apply these, color becomes almost impossible to grasp. It is not my intent to prescribe a perfect set of color palettes—color is a personal choice based on your own preferences and perceptions. In Chapter 7 we discuss the common color harmonies and ways to select color palettes that are harmonious. With these skills, you will be able to work virtually any color combination into your projects.

Personal choice should be at the forefront of color decisions, guided with information to make the choices rational. This book is but one journey you'll make in studying color. This book will provide all students of interior design with invaluable illustrations for learning and understanding color and design.

With effective color usage, an interior designer can manipulate our experiences in the built environment. Knowing this tremendous power and developing skill in how to use it gives the designer the ability to orchestrate the reactions of the inhabitants of interior space. This book presents a different approach to thinking about color and design that will enable to you become more informed and successful in your use of color. Color shapes behavior, behavior shapes culture, and culture shapes design. Our world is constantly changing, color is constantly changing, and approaches to design will forever evolve.

# acknowledgments

This project has been a both personally and professionally challenging and a growing process as a teacher and a writer. The life lessons learned from this project will forever shape my classroom and mentoring of young designers. This book would have never happened without the many people whose professional guidance and contributing ideas shaped an idea into the soul of this book. I am so grateful to the authors before me whose writings on color have provided me with a wealth of knowledge. You are a community of teachers and I've learned so much from you.

I thank the many students whose work is contained within. It is for you that I hope the pages unfold and enlighten you all to the wonder color can bring to our spaces.

I am so thankful and grateful to the team at Fairchild who have helped this project along: To Executive Editor Olga Kontias for believing in me and this project. To the creative magic of Erin Fitzsimmons, Barbara Barg Medley, Steven Stankiewicz, and the Fairchild art department, you were all truly amazing at making the art and illustrations materialize beautifully. Blessings to Editorial Development Director Jennifer Crane in providing extended periods during hectic schedules for me to provide the necessary attention for the book's development.

A special thank you to Liz Marotta for finessing the details and quality. I would especially like to thank Development Editor Michelle Levy for her unconditional support, encouragement, and patience. This project would never have happened without your guidance, and I am truly grateful for you.

I would also like to thank the many artists, interior and graphic designers, and architects whose work was contributed for their generosity in support of the project. To the reviewers, Kathryn Burton, Stephanie Clemons, and Sandra Gibbons, whose professional insights and suggestions were graciously offered, thank you.

And to my former professors and colleagues whose work has shaped and mentored my life as a designer and now as an educator, I am deeply thankful for each of you: Sylvan Eldringhoff, Katharine Leigh, Denise Bertoncino, and Dr. Jennifer Webb.

I want to express my heartfelt gratitude for my dearest friends who were loyal reminders of the book's progress and constant supporters throughout: Gaberial Rounds, Greg Fairchild, Dr. Keila Tyner, and Roy Solis.

And finally a special appreciation to my family; I am truly grateful to have each of you in my life.

# color + design

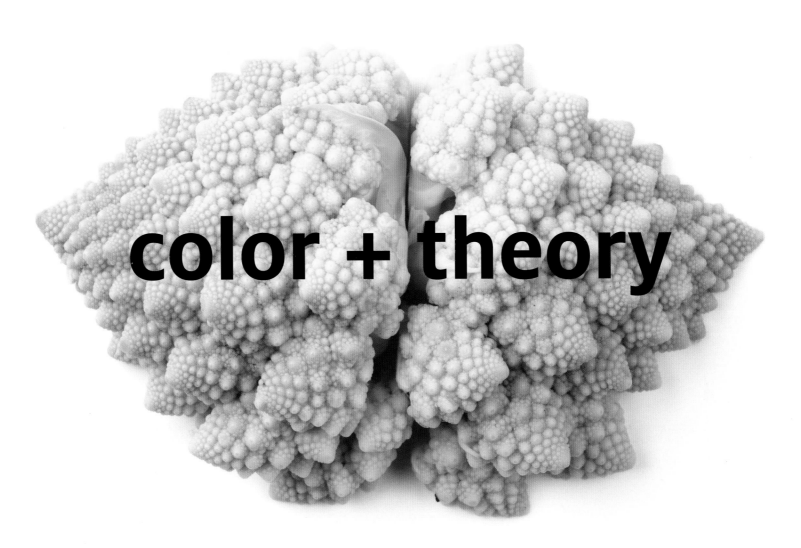

color + theory

Why do interior designers need to know about color? Color is an intangible, powerful sensation that has the ability to enhance our physical environment, influence our personal experiences of space, and provide a greater sense of health and well-being. Of all our senses, 80 percent of sensory experiences are visual. Color is unstable and constantly changing, which could exhaust a designer working with color matter. Our interaction with colored media—for instance, television, computer screens, and roadside billboards—can create an unexpected experience depending on the colors we are exposed to. We do not have control over these color sources, and the resulting emotional experiences are therefore uncertain. Unlike these media sources, our direct interaction with printed and colored materials including paint and fabrics allows for our complete control and choice of selection. Viewing colored media causes receptors in our eyes to transmit messages to our brain, which tries to give our experiences meaning. Color theorists have engaged in debates and discourse to explain the phenomena of color from Newton's first studies in the 1660s to Albers' work some 300 years later in the 1960s. Different professions require different approaches to interpret and express their ideas with color. A graphic designer works with printed color media, a theater lighting specialist works with colored light and light mixing, a painter brings a painting to life by mixing pigments, and an interior designer uses colored materials to intricately create spaces for his or her clients' desired outcomes. This complex process—color theory—has been studied for centuries. Color resists any one schematic system, which is why so many color theorists have spent countless hours trying to fit a square peg into a round hole. Designers rely more on instinct and experience than one theoretical color approach to guide them and gain confidence in working with color. Despite the many approaches, a basic understanding of color theory is fundamental to a well-rounded education in interior design.

Before we examine color theory more closely, let's first look at what is meant by *theory*. Theory explains the concepts and ideas involved in describing and rationalizing phenomena about a particular subject. Theories, for the most part, are unproven and continue to be studied to provide additional insight into the particular subject.

## WHAT IS COLOR THEORY?

Color theory is the study and practice of a set of principles used to understand the relationships among colors. Color theory has been studied for decades and new ideas and practices are continuously unraveled. The role color plays in art, design, and other allied professions is important to using color successfully. A certain amount of knowledge in the scientific aspects of color is necessary, however, from a design perspective; we are engaged in the human interface involving they way people respond to color. Whether in our homes, our offices, schools, or businesses, color transforms our surroundings.

## LET THERE BE LIGHT

Without light, there is no color. Color transforms as light is experienced. Light is the essence of color and is energy traveling through the air at 186,000 miles per second. Light and color together illuminate a space, guide focal point and attention, and set the mood and expression of the interior. Color materials and lighting types should be selected simultaneously to create harmony within the

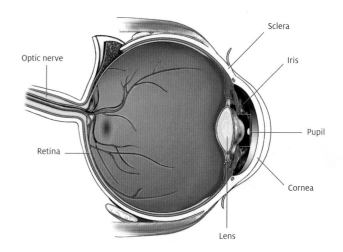

**FIGURE 1.1** Cross section of the human eye. The retina contains light sensitive nerve cells called cones and rods. (© PHOTOTAKE Inc./Alamy)

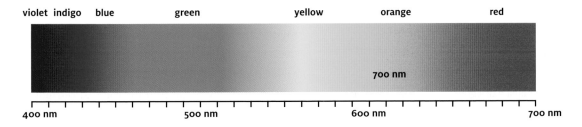

violet indigo blue    green    yellow    orange    red

700 nm

400 nm     500 nm     600 nm     700 nm

**FIGURE 1.2** The visible spectrum of colored light.

interior. If selected separately, the results can be disastrous. Color is a complex process resulting from light entering the eye where two types of light-sensitive nerve cells—**cones** (daylight/color receptors) and **rods** (dim light/value receptors)—within the retina transmit nerve impulses to the brain, resulting in color vision (Figure 1.1). There are three sets of cones sensitive to wavelengths of light: red, blue, and green.

Colored light consists of a series of wavelengths, each varying in length and strength. This colored light we can see is called the **visible spectrum** (Figure 1.2). The human eye is capable of seeing a very small portion of the electromagnetic spectrum, which consists of gamma rays, X-rays, ultraviolet light, infrared rays, microwaves, and radio waves (Figure 1.3).

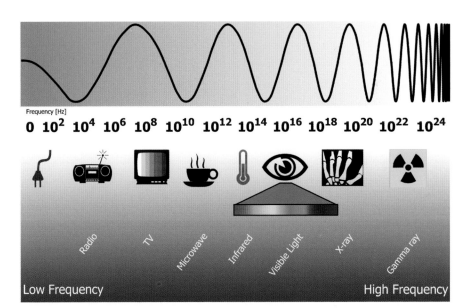

Frequency [Hz]

0  $10^2$  $10^4$  $10^6$  $10^8$  $10^{10}$  $10^{12}$  $10^{14}$  $10^{16}$  $10^{18}$  $10^{20}$  $10^{22}$  $10^{24}$

Radio    TV    Microwave    Infrared    Visible Light    X-ray    Gamma ray

Low Frequency                          High Frequency

**FIGURE 1.3** The electromagnetic spectrum. (© Friedrich Saurer/Alamy)

**TABLE 1.1** Wavelengths of Visible Light in Nanometers

| COLOR WAVELENGTHS | RANGE IN VISIBLE SPECTRUM (NM-NANOMETER) |
|---|---|
| Violet (400) | 390–455 (shortest wavelength) |
| Blue (475) | 455–492 |
| Green (510) | 492–577 |
| Yellow (570) | 577–597 |
| Orange (590) | 597–622 |
| Red (650) | 622–780 (longest wavelength) |

The visible portion of light we see is located between ultraviolet light and infrared light, approximately 390 to 780 **nanometers** (nm; 1 millimeter = 1 million nm), the unit used to describe and measure the wavelengths of visible light (see Table 1.1). Violet light has the shortest wavelength, whereas red has the longest. The longer the wavelength of light, the more effort the eye must make to see the object. Red light will focus behind the retina of the eye; green, the most pleasing color for the eye to view, on the retina; and violet slightly in front of the retina. The eye can have trouble focusing on violet, and it can have a "hazy" quality in large doses (Figure 1.4). Extensively red-colored space can be tiring and irritating if viewed for extended periods of time (Figure 1.5). It is recommended to use pure red in small doses, as an accent, or in locations where people visit for shorter periods. Tints and tones of this hue will not have the same effect.

Light reflects off surfaces, and, in fact, objects have no color of their own. Color is the result of light reflected off the surface of objects into the eye, resulting in color vision. The color of an object occurs from varying degrees of absorption of light energy, with the remaining light reflecting off the object into the eye, resulting in color vision (Figure 1.6). White-colored objects are absent of color, as they reflect all colored light. Black-colored objects are present of all color and therefore will absorb all colored light. Since light is heat, the absorption of colored light by black objects or other dark-colored object results in the absorption of this heat. White deflects the colored light and therefore is typically cool to the touch. An apple, for instance, is the result of all colored light being absorbed into the apple and only red light being reflected back into the eye. So, in a way, an apple isn't red, but every other color but red.

## PROPERTIES OF LIGHT

Three properties of light are commonly experienced in the design of the physical environment: reflection, diffraction, and refraction. **Reflection** occurs when light strikes an object, and in the case of seeing color, the light reflected back from an object results in the color we see. **Diffraction** occurs when light is partially obstructed by an object. This interference of the light bends the waves around the edges of object or opening and spreads outward, producing light, dark, or colored bands (Figure 1.7). Lastly, **refraction** results when one or more light rays moves through a light medium to another, denser medium such as air to water or a prism, causing light to bend (Figures 1.8 and 1.9). Colored light results in a prism and rainbow when light is slowed due to the material it is passing through. This reduced speed allows for the spectral colors to be seen by the human eye.

**FIGURE 1.4** Above. A suite at the Zetter Hotel in London incorporates a combination of violet finishes and lighting to create an ethereal, dreamlike quality resulting from the retina's inability to focus easily on this particular hue. (© VIEW Pictures Ltd/Alamy)

**FIGURE 1.5** Opposite page. Variations of the red light create a dramatic but potentially straining visual experience in the Toys "R" Us store in New York. (© James Leynse/Corbis)

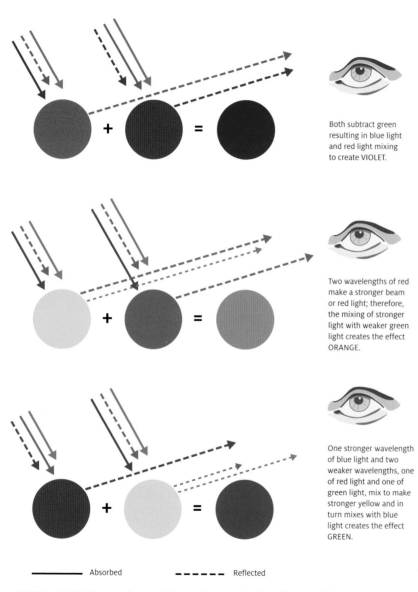

Both subtract green resulting in blue light and red light mixing to create VIOLET.

Two wavelengths of red make a stronger beam or red light; therefore, the mixing of stronger light with weaker green light creates the effect ORANGE.

One stronger wavelength of blue light and two weaker wavelengths, one of red light and one of green light, mix to make stronger yellow and in turn mixes with blue light creates the effect GREEN.

——— Absorbed    – – – – – Reflected

**FIGURE 1.6** This illustrates how red, blue, and green primaries of light (additive color theory) mix in relative strengths with one another when reflected off an object, resulting in the color we see.

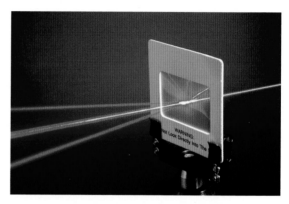

**FIGURE 1.7** Right. Red laser beam split by a diffraction grating. (© GIPhotoStock X/Alamy)

**FIGURE 1.8** Bottom. Refraction of a ray of light by a glass block.

(© sciencephotos/Alamy)

FIGURE 1.9 A seashell image in the water is disrupted by refracting light entering the water.

(© Stephen Frink/zefa/Corbis)

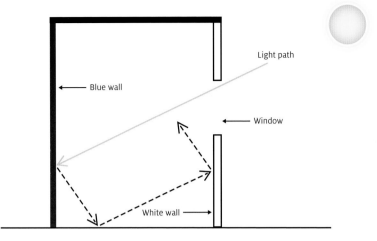

Light path

Blue wall

Window

White wall

FIGURE 1.10 The ray of sunlight passes through the window reflected off the blue wall; the color is then reflected onto other surfaces, leaving a slight blue cast. This reduces as the strength of daylight diminishes.

In Figure 1.9, the conch shell appears somewhat distorted due to the refracted light passing through the ocean water. **Direct color** results from viewing a color on a particular surface. **Indirect color** results from adjoining or opposite wall surfaces or objects reflecting their color. When light strikes one or more colored surfaces, the light will bounce throughout the space, impacting colored objects nearby. The reflected color mixes with other colored surface it's reflected onto or, in the case of a white wall, tints the surface with the reflected colored light (Figure 1.10). A blue-colored wall whose light is reflected onto oak flooring—a yellow-gold— will mix with the floor color, resulting in the floor appearing to have a tinge of green. Additionally, the more color light is reflected through the space, the less intense the colors become as it is dispersed. It is in this process that we will need to move away from the preconceived notion that you can "match" a color with other materials to look for the "acceptable match." While the mechanics of this

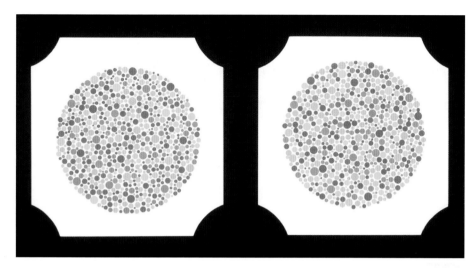

**FIGURE 1.11** Color blindness test plates. See if you can locate the numbers 5 and 7.
(Dorling Kindersley/Getty Images)

of these properties of light when using color in interiors. Each property offers its own unique spin to the way color can be perceived.

There are two basic types of color mixing: light and pigment. Additive color involves mixing light, and subtractive color mixes pigment.

### Additive Color

In **additive color**, the primary-light colors red, green, and blue are mixed. When these three colors of light are mixed or "added" together, white light is the result, and rationally, the absence of all colored light is black. In addition, when varying intensities of these lights are generated, multiple color combinations are possible. For instance, when the primaries overlap one another, the additive secondary colors are produced: Red light overlapping with blue results in magenta (bluish red), red overlapping with green produces yellow light, and blue light overlapping with green light produces cyan—a greenish blue (Figure 1.12).

### Subtractive Color

**Subtractive color** applies to paint, dyes, colorants, and inks, where blue, red, and yellow are identified as the primary colors; in printing and photography: cyan, magenta, and yellow (CMYK). The letter "K" stands for black. With subtractive mixing, the solid material we are viewing will absorb and reflect wavelengths of color. A red apple will absorb or "subtract out" all colored light and reflect the red wavelength of light back to the eye, resulting in the red apple we see. In reality, an apple isn't red, but rather all other colors of light. The combination of the subtractive primaries will result in the secondary colors violet, green, and orange. Further combination of varying degrees of secondary colors with each other and/or their respective primaries will result in a multitude of various color hues (Figure 1.13).

### The Many Faces of Color

The key factor that determines a color characteristic in the interior environment is the light source—an often-forgotten design element that can determine whether working with color is stressful or stress-free. I often see students labor over trying

process are necessary to understand the physical manifestation of color, the most important aspect to remember is not everyone sees color necessarily the same way despite this universal process. Whether the person is working with color for the first time or is a seasoned professional, he or she should be aware of the physical conditions that alter the visual perception of color. These include, but are not limited to, age, gender, aging health of the eye, personality, and forms of color blindness. In the United States, more men than women have color blindness. Color blindness is linked to the X chromosome. Men only have one, whereas women have two. It is rare in women to have both X chromosomes carry the anomaly. Approximately 1 out of 12 males have some form of **color blindness**, whereas 1 out of 20 females have color blindness (Morton, 2008). In the most common type of color blindness, red and green are perceived as being the same. As you can see in Figure 1.11, within each circle is a number; if you have difficulty seeing the number or can't see it at all, you may have a form of color blindness. You should see a "5" in the left circle and a "7" in the right circle. Consider each

to get or create the exact color they have in mind only to have it change in appearance in different lighting conditions. This phenomenon is referred to as **metamerism**. Avoid making color choices under one set of lighting conditions. Whether you're seeing the color during various times of the day, each resulting in different amounts of light, under incandescent or lamp light, fluorescent light, or during different seasonal lighting conditions, each will have a different effect on the perceived color of the object. Because natural light is sunlight, and thus pure light, it consists of all visible colors light, or white light. Any form of man-made light will vary in color rendition, from a small percentage to much greater, depending on the lighting type being used.

Let's look at an example. Suppose you are standing before hundreds of color choices in a showroom, and you think you've determined just the right colors for your project. You take the swatches home, and suddenly the blue no longer looks blue—it's now green. What happened? Did you pick up the wrong sample? This is an all-too-familiar incident for many people when selecting color swatches for upholstering new furnishings. We've become so accustomed to color, we don't even realize how complicated it can be, taking it for granted and assuming that it will always stay constant no matter how or where we decide to use it. Light is the key, since, after all, color *is* light, and many times we ignore light, not realizing it is more important than the color itself.

Color can be daunting to work with, offering a multitude of possibilities that often makes you feel like you are playing a game of roulette trying to find the perfect color palette. Because of the importance of light in selecting color, it is crucial to examine the color source in different lighting conditions. Color choices are mistakenly made in showrooms without clients ever seeing the color at home. Showrooms are typically illuminated with multiple light sources, including fluorescent bulbs. Artificial light sources never render the true color characteristics of fabrics, trims, paint, or wood tones. Fluorescent lights generally emit reddish (warm) or bluish (cool) light that will alter the true color of materials, and once the materials are placed within our homes, they will appear noticeably different. The color temperature, or **Kelvin**, of various lamp sources will determine the proper color

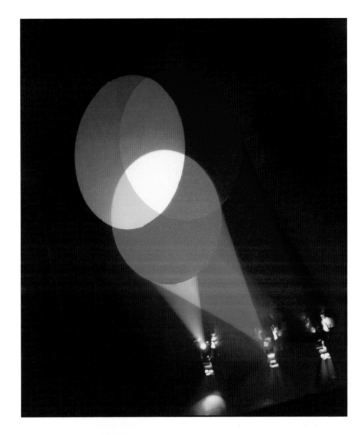

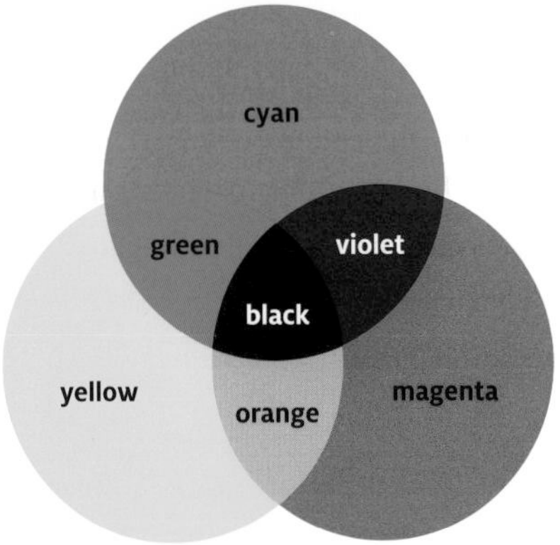

**FIGURE 1.12** Top. Additive color light mixing. (Fritz Goro/Time & Life Pictures/Getty Images)

**FIGURE 1.13** Left. Subtractive color process mixing.

rendition of matter under various lighting conditions. Kelvin is based on a numerical system where natural sunlight is generally noted at around 5,500 K and candlelight is around 1,500 K. A 40-watt incandescent lamp is around 2,680 K, and most incandescent lamps range from 2,600 to 3,100 K. Fluorescent lamps will have a color temperature around 4,100 K. Kelvin represents the full color range in the visible spectrum. The higher the Kelvin number, the cooler the temperature, and the lower the number, the warmer the temperature, relative to the color wavelengths mentioned earlier. The first two numbers represent the range of 0 to 100, with the second number indicating the Kelvin temperature to the nearest hundred. The **color rendering index** (CRI) indicates the light source's ability to render the true color of an object as it would appear in natural light using Kelvin to identify the color temperature. The higher the CRI index rating (80 or above), the less likely an individual color will vary in appearance from its appearance in sunlight.

Working with a knowledgeable lighting designer or lighting specialist will eliminate the guesswork concerning the characteristics of the many possible light sources. Following are a few tips to keep in mind:

- Showrooms typically provide **memo samples** of upholstery used in their furniture lines. These samples are large and show one or multiple repeats of the pattern design. Be sure not to work with small samples when making color decisions. The small samples are inadequate in representing the true color and pattern on furniture, drapery, walls, and so on. When possible, take the samples home and view the fabrics under the different light sources in the home. Examine the textile in morning, afternoon, and nighttime lighting conditions. The location in the room, time of day, and amount of natural sunlight reaching a particular area in your room, as well as the artificial lighting in the home, will all contribute to the many faces of the color. Generally speaking, neutrals and lighter tones will have a greater color change than darker tones. Neutral colors can have a remnant of other colors present that, when intensified by certain light sources, might result in a hint of the color coming through. For instance, perhaps you've had the experience where that lovely shade of antique-white paint you selected looked pink once applied to a wall.

- The surface characteristics of textiles, trims, and wood will also play a role in their perceived color. The color of highly textured surfaces will appear darker in value, and glossy surfaces will appear lighter. This is because of the amount of light that is reflected off the surface—the more light reflected, the brighter the color; the less light reflected, the darker the color. If you are attempting to match a color, surface texture is a key factor to your success. It will be difficult to match two items of the same color with different textures. At most, you can coordinate.

- When you are examining the color source at different times of the day and under different light sources to see how dramatically the color changes, also examine the source in different positions. If you are selecting a textile, lay the textile flat on the seat of a chair or sofa as well as vertically to examine how its color changes. Light reflects off vertical and horizontal surfaces differently, and color will vary accordingly. It is best to view your color selections in the location where they are intended to be used; otherwise, you run the risk of improper color selection and balancing with other colors in the room. The same principles apply to paint. It is better to buy a quart and paint a large (about 5 feet by 5 feet) area on your walls in different locations within the rooms and examine how much the color changes under various light sources and at different times of day. If using this technique, paint the sample area with the same finish that will be used on the walls (flat, eggshell, gloss); otherwise, the reflective qualities will change the paint color. Some designers paint the color onto pieces of white foam board or drywall to test the color before painting. Caution is needed if your walls are textured, since foam board is a smooth surface, which may cause the color to appear lighter.

- If you are a student at a school of design, check to see if you have a color viewing light-box. This tool incorporates various lighting sources where colored materials and products samples can be viewed to witness these color changes (Figure 1.14).

These tips will ensure that the color sources chosen do not change in such a way as to compromise the overall room design and will assist you in finding colors that are appealing to your sense of style. Color is complicated, but with some basic skills and a fearless attitude, you'll gain a greater sense of security to explore with color.

## Light Reflectance

**Light reflectance value (LRV)** refers to the percentage of light that is reflected from a colored surface back into the interior space. Paint manufactures provide light reflectance values ranging in percentage from 0 to 100 for their products. Zero has no reflectance value (black), and 100 reflects the most light (white). Take caution to avoid high reflectance values, as the glare can cause discomfort and eye fatigue. Avoid in places of extensive or continuous, such as surfaces in work environments. A good rule of thumb for residential spaces is anything within 50 percent LRV is generally acceptable. The amount of reflectance from vertical and horizontal surfaces and the interior finishes within must be taken into consideration. Ceilings need a reflectance value between 60 and 90 percent, walls between 30 and 60 percent, and floors between 15 and 35 percent. In spaces where task lighting is needed versus ambient lighting, these numbers should increase approximately 10 percent in reflectance value.

Surface characteristics add to the visual perception of colored matter. Surfaces that are reflective weaken the apparent color, whereas textured surfaces strengthen the perceived darkness of color, particularly due to the shadows that are created in this process. There are varying degrees of reflected qualities of surfaces, and much like the value scale, the textural qualities of these surfaces will change the perceived lightness or darkness of a color (Figure 1.15). The most common time interior designers consider properties of reflection is when working with paints—when the choice of flat, eggshell, satin, semigloss, and gloss sheens are available. If there is too much glare in the surface material, it will be difficult to see the color.

## COLOR SYSTEMS

Color theorists study and explain the characteristics of color creations, interactions, and arrangements. Many theorists and authors have spent years researching

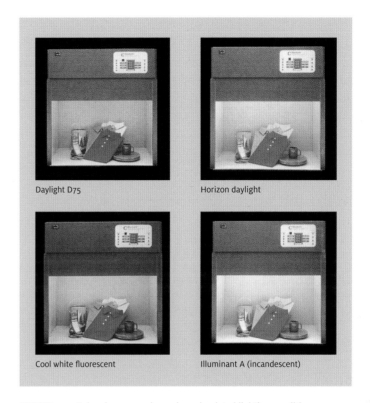

Daylight D75

Horizon daylight

Cool white fluorescent

Illuminant A (incandescent)

**FIGURE 1.14** Color changes under various simulated lighting conditions.

High gloss surface

Satin surface finish

Matt or flat finish

Textured surface reflection

**FIGURE 1.15** Surface texture reflection characteristics.

**TABLE 1.2** Chronological History of Twelve Works on Color Theory

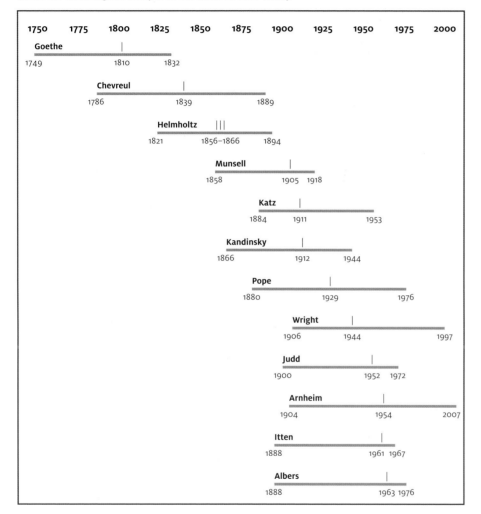

| 1750 | 1775 | 1800 | 1825 | 1850 | 1875 | 1900 | 1925 | 1950 | 1975 | 2000 |
|---|---|---|---|---|---|---|---|---|---|---|

Goethe
1749    1810    1832

Chevreul
1786    1839    1889

Helmholtz
1821    1856–1866    1894

Munsell
1858    1905   1918

Katz
1884    1911    1953

Kandinsky
1866    1912    1944

Pope
1880    1929    1976

Wright
1906    1944    1997

Judd
1900    1952   1972

Arnheim
1904    1954    2007

Itten
1888    1961   1967

Albers
1888    1963   1976

**FIGURE 1.16** Top. Sir Isaac Newton analyzing the colors refracted from light through a prism. Left. Colored light refracted through a prism. (Top: © North Wind Picture Archives/Alamy; left: © Peter Arnold, Inc./Alamy)

color and providing systems to aid those interested in expanding their knowledge and increasing their confidence in using color. An entire book could be dedicated to delving into the historical developments of color systems. The complexities alone are addressed in a series of books. No single system has been identified as ideal for interior design. Over the last three centuries, there have been 12 books considered "crucial to the study of color" (Burchett, 2005, p. 91), starting as early as 1749 with the works of Goethe. A chronological history of these 12 works is presented in Table 1.2. For this book, we will look at those systems that are more commonly known and referred to today in design education and practice.

## Isaac Newton

Several theoretical approaches and interpretation of the color wheel have been developed since Sir Isaac Newton's work was published in 1666. Between 1664 and 1666, Newton developed his theory of color and delivered his findings in a lecture series conducted between 1670 and 1672. His work on color theory was later produced in his book *Opticks.* Newton was more interested in the physics of color and is known for having discovered refracted colors—a phenomenon that results when light passes through a prism (Figure 1.16). He developed the first of what would later become many color wheels, which consisted of the visible color of the spectrum (primary and secondary) constructed with their relative proportions, as seen when colored light is refracted (Figure 1.17).

## Albert H. Munsell

American born Munsell (1858–1918) developed the most widely used color system, known as the "color tree" (Figure 1.18). His book *A Color Notation* (1905) has become a must-read in art and design schools. Munsell was credited for developing the three dimension of color: hue, value, and chroma (saturation). **Hue** (pure color) is the property of light by which the color of an object is classified as red, blue, green, or yellow in reference to the visible spectrum. Hue is expressed in the "branches" of the color tree. Munsell's color tree consists of ten hues. Each hue in the color trees is assigned a letter and numerical notation: 5R (red), 5YR (yellow-red), 5Y (yellow), 5GY (green-yellow), 5G (green), 5BG (blue-green), 5B (blue),

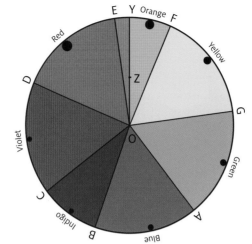

**FIGURE 1.17** Left. Newton color wheel.

**FIGURE 1.18** Bottom. Munsell color tree system.

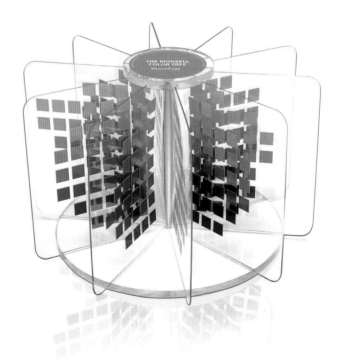

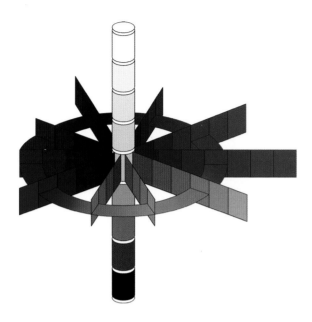

**FIGURE 1.19** Munsell color space.

## Josef Albers

Josef Albers (1888–1976) was a German-born artist who taught at the Bauhaus School of Art, which was founded by Walter Gropius and operated between 1919 and 1933. Albers is notably credited with his work in color relationships published in his book *Interaction of Color* in a series of well-known pieces of artwork (Figure 1.20). Albers's work investigates illusions of color using colored paper—a

**FIGURE 1.20** *Homage to Square: Terra Caliente* by Josef Albers, 1964. (© Albright-Knox Art Gallery/Corbis)

5PB (purple-blue), 5P (purple), 5RP (red-purple). The number 5 represents the center of the color family, where each color is at its purist. **Value** refers to the lightness or darkness of a color. Munsell identifies value on a scale of 0 to 10, with pure white at the top for 0, gray in the middle for 5, and black at the bottom for 10. Value is expressed in the "trunk" of the tree. **Chroma** refers to the purity of a color, completely absent of any white, gray, or black that would lessen its intensity or saturation, two additional terms acceptable for describing the color strength. Chroma is represented by the horizontal scale on the color tree (Figure 1.19). As you move up the trunk and outward, the hues become lighter in value. As you move down the trunk and outward, the hues become darker. The closer you are to the trunk with any given hue, the less saturated the color; the farther out on the branches, the more pure the color will be.

material that is easily available, inexpensive compared to electronic color media, and commonly used in design school today. After the closure of the Bauhaus school, Albers immigrated to the United States in 1933, where he began teaching color theory at Black Mountain College until 1949. Albers moved to Connecticut, and from 1950 to 1959, he was the chairman of the Department of Design at the Yale University School of Art (Droste, 2006, p. 242). Since designers are constantly working with color media, his work is of importance when you need to quickly investigate color manipulation and changes. His interactions are explained further in Chapter 2.

## Johannes Itten

Johannes Itten (1888–1967) was a Swiss-born painter, textile designer, and teacher of color theory. Itten began teaching at the Bauhaus 1919 and left in 1923 due to conflicts with Walter Gropius over his teaching methods (Froebel Web, ¶ 7). Itten wrote several books on color theory including *The Elements of Color* and *The Art of Color*. Itten developed the 12-pointed color star (Figure 1.21) where he primarily explored contrast, most notably cold-warm contrasts. Itten was the first to explore color expressed through shape and form using astrological, cultural traditions, and symbols that have greatly influenced our perception of color and shape. His theory is explained further in Chapter 2.

## Faber Birren

American-born Faber Birren (1900–1988) attended the University of Chicago from 1920 to 1921, where he studied color theory. At the age of 30, Birren moved to New York to work as a color consultant. Birren is well known for publishing 25 books on color, beginning with *Color in Vision* in 1928. His most notable pieces of work—*Principles of Color, Color, and Human Response* and *Light, Color, and Environment*—are still used in art and design schools today. Birren was one of the first color theorists to recognize the human condition in terms of biological and psychological responses to color. His research focus involved the changing physical environment and the emotional characteristics of its inhabitants.

**FIGURE 1.21** *The Color Star* by Johannes Itten. (Wiley Publications)

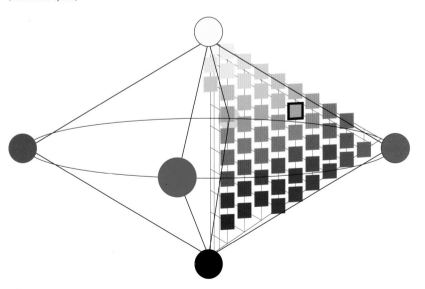

**FIGURE 1.22** (a) Top. NCS color circle—40 hues. (b) Bottom. NCS color triangle.

(Natural Color System)

**color + theory**

## Natural Color System® (NCS®)

The Natural Color System originated in Switzerland in the 1920s. Originally founded in 1946 and called The Color Institute, its current name was established in 1978. NCS is currently represented in 22 countries and is one of the mostly widely used international systems for color communication among designers and architects. The NCS offers a variety of educational tools for students and teachers of color theory. The most notable element is their 40-hue color circle using red, blue, green, and yellow as its distinctive primaries, with 9 intermediate steps between each (Figure 1.22a). This is further subdivided into a color triangle for each hue with 53 individual color separations (Figure 1.22b). The educational tools provide students with a multitude of color samples to explore various visual manipulations of color. Several of the exercises represent the work of Albers and Itten. Information on purchasing these materials is available on the Web at www.ncscolour.com.

## Pantone®

Pantone was created in 1943 as a tool for color management, matching, identification, and communication of color to produce color more accurately. Pantone is currently used in the retail, fashion, graphic arts, paint, interiors, and product development. It offers a variety of media to use for color specification and selection, including cotton swatch charts, color charts, colored plastics, and design books, to name a few. Information about Pantone is available on the Web at www.pantone.com.

## Color-aid®

The Color-aid system is a colored-paper system developed in 1948 and used extensively by Josef Albers. The system consists of 314 colors with 34 vivid hues (saturated colors), 100 tints (clean, light colors), 47 shades (dark, deep colors), 114 pastels (muted or soft colors), and 17 grays from dark to light, plus black and white organized to reflect the Munsell system. The matte-finish samples are offered in sizes ranging from 2 by 3 inches to 6 by 9 inches (Figure 1.23). This

**FIGURE 1.23** Color-aid system composed of 314 hues, including pure hue, tints, tones, and shades. (Color-aid)

system can be an invaluable tool for design students who will eventually work with color charts and decks for color selection.

### Electronic Media

A variety of printing techniques and computer applications that expand on these various systems are used in the communication design industry. In the visualization of interiors, these systems are limited in function and convenience. Computer screens and television technology use the additive theory RBG, or red, blue, and green, light for color mixing. CYMK is another system composed of cyan, yellow, magenta, and black. While these systems do have their place in working with color, the common problem is the difference that results between the

colors viewed on a screen (light) and the printed paper (pigment); the designer must always keep in mind that pixels aren't the same as paint. This can be seen when students use various manufacturers' online sample programs for specifying materials and finishes. Students are often confused when they've selected a fabric, paint, or solid surface material for a project online only to receive the sample through the mail and realize that the color appearance is different than the screen sample. Since designers in practice commonly work with actual materials, color charts, samples, paints, dyed materials, and various colorants, the use of computer for color management is limited in value to the designer. However, as computer technology continues to advance and use within design firms increases, this may very well change.

### COLOR LANGUAGE

In addition to hue, value, and chroma, there are several terms that are used to describe the various qualities of color. A clear understanding of each will ensure clarity among users of color. You can change color three ways: through tint, tones, and shades. Adding any amount of white to a color produces a **tint**, such as pink. Adding gray to a color (mixture of black and white) produces a **tone** such as the color puce. Adding black to a color results in a **shade**, such as burgundy. A **pure hue** is a color void of any white, gray, or black and is at its highest intensity or brightness, such as red (Figure 1.24). **Chromatic** refers to all colors minus black,

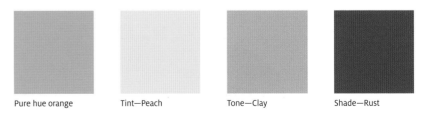

Pure hue orange    Tint—Peach    Tone—Clay    Shade—Rust

**FIGURE 1.24** The colored square on the far left is the pure hue for orange. In each of the proceeding squares, the original hue has been modified with white, then gray, then black to show the changes that occur in the purity of the orange color.

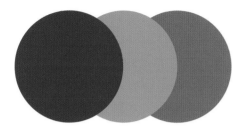

**FIGURE 1.25** Split complementary.

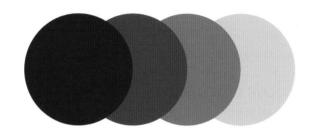

**FIGURE 1.26** Monochromatic.

**FIGURE 1.27** Triad.

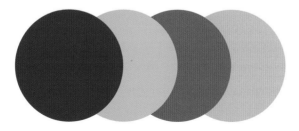

**FIGURE 1.28** Tetrad.

white, and gray. **Achromatic** refers to black, white, and gray, each of which is without color. **Primary hues** are red, blue, and yellow. Each color cannot be produced by any combination of the three. **Secondary hues** are violet, green, and orange, each made from combining two primaries. **Tertiary hues** are red-violet, blue-violet, blue-green, yellow-green, yellow-orange, and red-orange, each made by combining a secondary hue with one of the primaries.

**Complementary** colors result from two colors opposite one another on the color wheel: red/green, blue/orange, and violet/yellow. **Analogous** color schemes result from two or more colors adjacent to one another on the color wheel: blue/blue-green/green. Commonly, three to four colors constitute a pleasing analogous scheme by allowing a wider range of colors to harmonize. Any less or any more color can be monotonous or overwhelming. A **split complementary** color scheme is similar to the complementary scheme; however, it's composed of three colors consisting of one main hue plus the two hues each adjacent to its complement—for example, blue, red-orange, and yellow-orange (Figure 1.25). A **monochromatic** color scheme is based on variations of particular hue (Figure 1.26). **Triad** color schemes are composed of three colors equally spaced along the color wheel (Figure 1.27). **Tetrad** color schemes are composed of four colors equally spaced along the color wheel (Figure 1.28). Cool colors are blues, greens, and blue-violets. Warm colors are red, red-violets, yellow, and oranges (Figure 1.29). Notice that brown has been left out of the discussion thus far. Brown is the only hue that is not part of the color wheel. Mixing orange, red, and small amounts of black result in the hue brown; variations of this hue can be achieved by adding more black (dark brown) or white (tan). Another method for creating brown is by mixing complementary colors, red and green, blue and orange, and yellow and violet (Figure 1.30).

In this chapter we've presented the systems most commonly referenced and used in the design industry and the foundations of color theory applicable to interior space. To expand your knowledge, you might want to research the following individuals: Wilhelm Ostwald, Frans Gerritsen, and Johann Wolfgang von Goethe In addition, the appendix provides a historical timeline tracking the chronological evolution of the use of colored mattered using colorants and dyes.

## KEY WORDS

cones, rods, visible spectrum, nanometers, reflection, diffraction, refraction, direct color, indirect color, color blindness, additive color, subtractive color, metamerism, Kelvin, color rendering index, memo samples, light reflectance value (LRV), hue, value, chroma, tint, tone, shade, pure hue, chromatic, achromatic, primary hues, secondary hues, tertiary hues, complementary, analogous, split complementary, monochromatic, triad, tetrad

## LEARNING OUTCOMES

- Hue, value, and chroma are the three dimensions of color.
- Additive color theory applies to combining the three primaries of light—red, blue, and green.
- Subtractive color theory applies to combining the three primaries of pigment—red, blue, and yellow.
- A variety of color systems are available to designers. No single solution is used in the interior design industry; rather, each system offers its own contribution to learning about and working with color.

## EXERCISES

1. Observe your surroundings and look for examples of the three qualities of light mentioned in the chapter (reflection, refraction, diffraction). Take several photographs of the phenomena, and write brief descriptions of what you experience and see.
2. Using Color-aid paper, generate a ten-step incrementally distributed value scale similar to Munsell.
3. Produce the 5R value scale for hue red and the six-step chroma scale for red using Munsell's color tree. Use Color-aid paper to produce the value and chroma, and create a separate value and chroma scale using red-dyed or printed textiles. Using the two different media will challenge you to find the color sequence with the added texture and light reflectance of the textile.

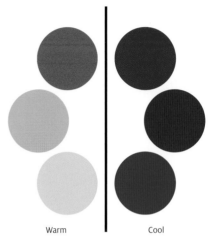

**FIGURE 1.29** Primary and secondary hues showing the division of warm and cool colors.

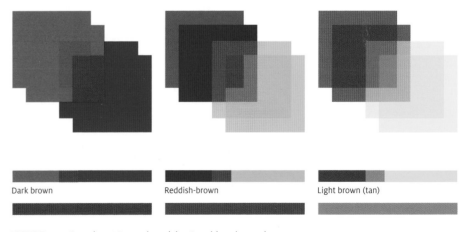

Dark brown        Reddish-brown        Light brown (tan)

**FIGURE 1.30** Complementary color mixing to achieve brown hues.

# color +
# psychology +
# perception

## 2

Just as water is necessary for life, color sustains our souls. Color is emotionally subjective. Factors that drive interior designers in color selection include trends, styles, and aesthetics; behavior and emotions; symbolic meaning based on age, gender, and cultural differences; pragmatic value—what the space needs to work well; and personal preference. We've become so preoccupied with color that we lose sight of simply enjoying it for what it is. However one approaches the study of color, whether quantitatively or intuitively, success as an interior designer depends on one's choice and expression.

The psychological associations and perception we have of color space can be a fascinating genre of design to explore in your work. The information represents the most common types of responses, but individual reactions to color stimuli vary from person to person.

## COLOR ASSOCIATIONS AND PERCEPTIONS

Scientific experiments have shown that humans can discriminate between very subtle differences in color, and estimates of the number of colors we can see range as high as 7 to 10 million. Rudolph Arnheim describes our visual perception of color as a process where the eye doesn't "record each of the infinitely many shades of hue by a particular kind of message but limits itself to a few fundamental colors, or ranges of color, from which all the others are derived . . . a kind of abstraction by which, at the level of conscious perception, we see colors as variations and combinations of a few primaries" (1969, p. 21). He goes on to explain that the millions of colors we can potentially see would be "unmanageable" when distinguishing colored objects and our brain must process and screen the large amount of information into a simple "order" to be able to adequately respond to the visual stimulation we encounter daily (p. 22).

Color response is highly personal. What one person is attracted to, another may be repulsed by. There is no such thing as a bad color—only unpleasant color relationships. We use color to describe our emotions and feelings. Color meanings and usage will vary from culture to culture. Color associated with certain objects or shapes can produce strong psychological responses. For instance, a favorite toy as a child, a memorable birthday present, or a holiday symbol can have positive associations that you carry with you. A family heirloom that was handed down from generation to generation may create a positive connection with its color. The opposite can be true for colors you may not like; a traumatic event in your life may be associated with a particular color. When you consider the colors you like or dislike, think about why you feel this way versus accepting the emotional reaction. This is valuable when talking with clients about color for a specific project.

Some crayon color names have led to negative associations, such as flesh, Prussian blue, and indian red. These color names were deemed offensive by civil rights groups and later changed to more appropriate names: peach, midnight blue, and chestnut (Crayola, 2008, ¶ 3–4). Tests conducted on color and emotions resulted in "yellow, blue, and orange as happy colors and red, black, and brown as sad colors" (Singh, 2006, p. 785). The basic colors (primary and secondary) trigger their own unique responses when viewed in isolation or in combination. These associations will vary depending on the context of their use within the built environment.

As mentioned in the introduction, the Department of Homeland Security introduced a color-coded, threat-based advisory system to alert the public of potential safety threats. This five-step system uses color to inform Americans of the countries current threat level. The colors advance from green (low), blue (guarded), yellow (elevated), orange (high), and red (severe) (Figure 2.1).

## COLOR AND HEALTH

Color can affect our brainwaves, emotions, and biological systems. Colored surfaces and colored light have the ability to increase and decrease heart rate, blood pressure, respiratory rate, and body temperature, and can be used to treat cancer, depression, and bacterial infections. The full spectrum of daylight is needed to stimulate our endocrine systems properly.

Color therapy, or **chromo therapy**, is the "practice of using colored light and color in the environment to cure specific illness and in general to bring about

**FIGURE 2.1** Department of Homeland Security Advisory System. (U.S. Department of Homeland Security)

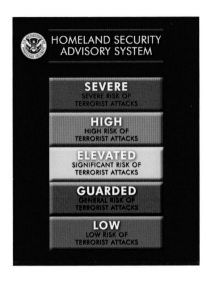

will begin to strain the eye, sending messages of confusion and discomfort to the brain. Observation is the key to learning. Pay attention to your moods for a short period of time, and notice the color of the environment and light sources present within the space.

## COLOR RESPONSES

Emotional reponses to color cannot be simply measured or limited just to any one particular hue. Color's effect on mood is ever changing as perceptions of our environment change. Color isn't seen in isolation, and, therefore, most of our visual responses occur as a result of the combination of colors, color in context with the immediate surroundings, and the interplay of light and texture as well as shape. Color perception is affected by individual associations of color. This is affected by culture, society, politics, entertainment/media, fashion, and design trends.

Our experience of color can be categorized in one of four experiences: the luminosity or saturation of the hue (bright/dull, light/dark), the color as it relates to a particular object to which we've assigned emotional attachment, our emotional response to a particular color (like or dislike), and the character or mood a color expresses to a particular observer. The latter is often the result of social and cultural biases that have imprinted these characteristics into our psyche, along with the media through television, the Internet, and magazines.

The color mauve, a muted blue-violet, was fashionable in interiors during the late 1980s, in contrast to the garish avocado green and harvest gold of the 1970s. The color was introduced on the runways, where most color trends are introduced; however, as fashion and consumer attitudes have changed, this color is not currently considered attractive but rather out-of-fashion (Figure 2.2). Key to remember is that colors do not change, only our acceptance of them over time. However, the Color Marketing Group has indicated the potential return of a renewed mauve as one of the color trends for 2009. The color will be reintroduced with greater emphasis on the "dusty violet tones" (2008, ¶ 10). New color tastes originate from the fashion industry and slowly trickle down into home décor. A

beneficial health effect" (Hope and Walch, 1990, p. 75). Color therapy is a rather a new science in the United States and is not well understood; however, within the past 20 years, its popularity has increased as we move from speculation to understanding because of positive results observed in patients. Historically, ancient Egypt and certain Asian cultures' use of color as a healing tool were common. Our bodies are like prisms; we absorb white light and, thus, all colors. Difficulty in breathing can be offset by natural light filtered through yellow glass. Migraine headaches can be treated with sunlight filtered through blue glass. Depression has been known to be treated with red light, and nervousness and irritability with blue light. A sore throat can be eased with the use of green light. Individuals who have lost their sight can have their mood affected by the transmission of colored light, releasing a hormone in the hypothalamus that controls mood (Hope and Walsh, 1990, p. 75).

Fatigue can occur due to extended periods of visual exposure to strong colors, such as pure red or yellow, despite their properties of being colors that induce excitement and energy. Much like loud music from a concert, certain stimuli can have negative impacts on our body's energy level from overexposure. These colors color trend typically has a seven-year life span with four phases. It takes approximately one to two years for the colors to enter the marketplace, commonly in fashion first, sparking an interest. This is followed by a three- to five-year period where it is seen as popular, and it becomes available in textiles and decorative items from your local retailers. Then during the final six- to seven-year period, the colors begin to lose consumer interest and are replaced with a different hue or one evolved from the previously popular hue. An example is burgundy, popular in the early 1990s, to a rusty-orange red popular in the late 1990s, to the now red-orange, a more vibrant version of its original predecessors.

Color preferences are generally listed in the order of blue, red, green, violet, orange, and yellow. Blue is the first choice of Western cultures. In Japan, red is ranked as the favorite color. In Chapter 9 we explore cultural color perceptions, symbolism, and meanings. Nationally, white replaces silver in 2008 as the preferred car color. Age and gender can have an impact on color perception. Newborns at first can only see contrast between light and dark—the first hue to be recognizable is yellow because it is the most luminous of colors. Children in grade school grow out of yellow and show a stronger preference in adolescence to red and blue. In older adults, a shift occurs toward blues and greens. With aging of the eye and yellowing of the lens of the eye, there is a stronger need for the color blue.

Preferences for color can be associated with geographical regions and historic traditions. Red is alluring and striking, drawing people into a positive selling environment; however, it can make people feel tense. Bright, warm colors tend to produce quick impulse-buying. Soft, cool colors tend to encourage deliberation and are best used on costly purchases where consumers are encouraged to stay longer before making a decision. Product packaging should catch the consumers' eye first. Research indicates that consumers scan each package on a supermarket shelf for only three hundredths of a second (Machin, 2005, ¶17). Thus, the packaging must attract the customer to buy it, and the color should also help convey an image of the contents. If I were to ask you to walk down the supermarket isle and pick up a box of Cheerios® or Campbell's® soup, you would easily be able

**FIGURE 2.2** Living room with popular mauve and pink colors during the 1980s. (© Michael Crockett; Elizabeth Whiting & Associates/Corbis)

to find the product among the many options available simply by color recognition. Our perception of color influences our desire for a product. Bottled water manufacturers use clear or blue-tinted plastic to make the water appear more refreshing. If they suddenly decided to place water in brown bottles, the public perception might be the water is dirty. Red, yellow, and orange draw attention most; purple is associated with luxury; blue suggests cleanliness and/or quietness; green suggests nature; and gold, silver, and black are effective in promoting high-quality merchandise.

Insects displaying yellow and black markings warn potential predators to stay away, including the Monarch butterfly, coral snake, and poison dart frog (Figure 2.3). Colors that are used on road signs to alert drivers, when used in interior spaces, may elicit negative responses, including tension, increase in heart rate, nervousness, and fear.

Recent literature indicates that men prefer cool colors, whereas women prefer warm colors. Other studies have shown that color preference is very similar between the sexes; the only difference is that men tend to favor orange over yellow and woman favor yellow over orange (Khouw, 2007, ¶ 3).

## COLOR MYTHS AND BIASES

We are socially conditioned to believe that infant boys must wear blue and girls wear pink, and somewhere along the historical timeline, yellow became gender-neutral for either sex. It is so commonplace, we don't even question it. Preconceptions about color have led to several misconceptions about color. Gender bias for color didn't begin until the twentieth century and didn't acquire conformity until the 1950s. Historically, pink was favored and used for boys and blue for girls. Pink originates from red, which was and still is considered a powerful, strong color suitable that is preferred for young boys (colourlovers.com, 2007, ¶ 9–13).

Color carries no inherent message, but we superimpose our ideas on it. Society, media, and social and political issues are all factors that inevitably endow us with biases; we don't question, they are automatic. The world is colored, and for the most part, people have little control over the color they encounter day to day.

**FIGURE 2.3** Top left. Monarch butterfly colorations signal danger to predators. Right. Striped coral snakes are protected by black, red, and yellow skin pigments that warn predators of potential danger. Bottom left. The poison dart frog uses yellow and black coloring to warn potential predators to stay away. (Top left: © Pete Turner/Getty Images; right: Getty Images/Visuals Unlimited; bottom left: National Geographic/Getty Images)

These decisions are made by others—often by interior designers—and we interact with our environment either positively or negatively based on our perceived notions of particular colors.

The first writing tool a child will use is likely a Crayola crayon. Even in this instance the color names are taken from the U.S. Commerce Department's National Bureau of Standards book called *Color: Universal Language and Dictionary of Names.* Many crayon names are also borrowed from traditional artists' paints such as burnt sienna and raw umber. Americans' favorite Crayola crayon color is blue. As a child, coloring is one of our first interactions with and control over a variety of hues.

Over time, our preferences for colors change. Research on gender preference and color has indicated most men found red, then purple and pink as the most stimulating and blue as the most appealing when they were experiencing stress. "Men are more tolerant for neutrals hues such as black, white and gray than women" (Singh, 2006, p. 785). "Pink is used to calm violent prisoners in jails. The color suppresses anger, antagonistic, and anxiety-ridden behavior among prisoners: Even if a person tries to be angry or aggressive in the presence of pink, he can't. The heart muscles can't race fast enough. It's a tranquilizing color that zaps your energy." (Color Matters, 2008, ¶ 2). However, a study conducted in 1979 concluded that when prisoners were left in pink-painted jail cells for extended periods of time, they became "violent and out of control" (Uribes, 2008, ¶ 14).

The question for designers to consider is how does pink affect the mood of young girls or teens whose rooms are painted pink because social norms tell them that is what is appropriate? People are more productive in blue rooms, and studies show weightlifters are able to handle heavier weights in blue gyms.

Another popular color myth is the bias toward red vehicles. A common misconception among drivers is that red cars will received more speeding tickets than cars of other colors. Red has been associated with sports cars and speed. "There's also the supposed optical illusion created by their color that makes the cars appear to be going faster than they really are" (Edmunds Inc., 2008, ¶ 7). In actuality, according to Carolyn Gorman, vice president of the Insurance Information Institute and Insurance Trade Association, "there is no data to support the assertion that red cars receive more traffic tickets than cars of any other color" (Edmunds Inc., 2008, ¶ 7).

This phenomenon with the color red has been used by interior designers to influence individuals' perception of the passage of time. Red has been shown to increase the perception of time, whereas blue decreases the perceived amount of time spent. Red is commonly used in fast-food restaurants to indicate quick, speedy service, and casinos use red in the interior to excite and trick patrons into believing they have not spent much time in the space. Darker reds used in restaurants are intended to make customers spend more time, and in doing so, they are likely to spend more money for a dessert, wine, and a full-course meal. Blue and purple commonly used as appetite suppressants could fare well for an "all-you-can-eat" buffet where limiting the amount of return trips of its customers can save the restaurant money (Singh, 2006, p. 785).

Design research yielded statistical data that can be confidently used for evidence-based design decisions. Birren terms this "functional color," where the outcomes of color usage are based on the practical versus decorative uses of color (1992, p. 242). Solid research findings support your design decisions and can be used to add value and truth to your work. Table 2.1 expands on the common myths and biases with additional perceptual properties of color, including common positive associations, negative associations, healing properties, and consumer behaviors associated with particular hues.

## COLOR DESIGN PROCESS

Whether for residential or commercial spaces, color is a critical element and must be considered in the beginning of the design process. Color, as an element of design, is often studied separately and independently of the theories for design composition (principles and elements) due to its complexity. In a study on integrating color as part of the interior design process, Dianne Smith surveyed interior designers and architects on the need to be educated in color before entering design practice. Of those surveyed, 81 percent were educated in color and 88 percent integrated color as a design tool. The majority of color section occurred during the early stages of the design process, 44 percent occurring at the concept generation, and 56 percent during the schematic design phase (2003, p. 363).

Figure 2.4 diagrams the relationship between color, interior design, the principles and elements of design, and the design specialty. This model suggests examining color, at the center of all interior design decisions, with the elements of design (shape, line, form, and texture) and the principles of design (balance, rhythm, emphasis, proportion and scale, unity and harmony, and variety). The design process as presented by Kilmer and Kilmer (1992) identifies the eight steps designers use during project implementation. These include committing to the design problem, stating the design problem to be solved, collecting data, analyzing data, ideation of potential design solutions, choosing a final solution,

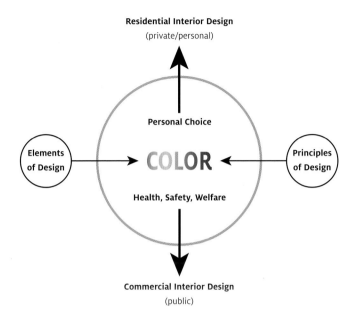

Residential Interior Design
(private/personal)

Personal Choice

Elements
of Design

COLOR

Principles
of Design

Health, Safety, Welfare

Commercial Interior Design
(public)

**FIGURE 2.4** Color application to design practice model.

implementing the design, and evaluating the final results (pp. 156–157). During this process, color is recommended to be filtered through each design stage. Rather than being a last-minute design decision or for decorative purposes only, a research-driven, holistic approach to color can help you achieve greater success in your designs.

Our homes are private spaces where we make personal choices that ultimately affect our living environment. At the opposite end, you have commercial spaces (health care, work spaces, retail, hospitality, and so forth) as public domains, which require more informed decisions about color use and application. These color decisions have the ability to affect the health, safety, and welfare of our clients and the multiple users of these spaces. We will break down the color components that invoke perceptual, emotional, and symbolic associations in the remainder of the text.

## COLOR AND SPACE

Color interactions in three-dimensional spaces have the ability to affect the size, shape, mass, and volume of interiors. Color is a key component in forming our first impressions of space and place. Color as a component of all materials of the environment—furniture, accessories, lighting, structure, plants, and more—can be used to communicate and express boundaries of space, visually connect architectural elements, and form the properties of the mood or atmosphere desired. Like time, we do not stand still; we are constantly moving through space, and therefore our experience is multifaceted and multisensory. Color speaks to us, helping us navigate and understand the visually complex world around us. The shape of an object conveys little without color to clarify its meaning and is not an "extra to an environmental situation but instead has an active role in the . . . relationship between a person and the surrounding environment" (Smith, 2007, p. 316).

Color and shape change as our locations and positions change. The interplay between color and space, lighting, and materials is experienced through all our senses. The power and propensity for color to be one of the first properties of our space we experience and therefore inform our environment is limitless. We simultaneously begin to make associations and emotional judgments on the space we have just encountered. These emotional judgments are reactionary based on our visual perceptions. Our immediate responses to our environment include, but are not limited to, recognizing the space type through design cues such as a bright-colored retail store front to indicate point of access, or a seating group organized around a reception station indicating a public space (waiting room or lobby). How we may perceive different space types will determine first impressions (like or dislike), greatly influenced by the color palette and materials chosen. For instance, when you enter a retail establishment, color is often the first cue to indicate what type of clothing section you are in. The children's clothing section is indicated with pale, pastel colors of pink and blue, the women's in light hues of violet, green, and turquoise, and the men's clothing section with darker hues of blue, gray, and black. Color cues make it easier to locate where you need to be with very little effort. If all sections within a retail environment were the same color, how quickly would you be able to locate items in the space?

**TABLE 2.1** Perceptual Properties and Association of Common Colors

| HUE | POSITIVE ASSOCIATIONS | NEGATIVE ASSOCIATIONS | HEALTH | CONSUMER BEHAVIOR |
|---|---|---|---|---|
| **RED** | Courage, excitement, love, passion, sexy, increases appetite, festivity (holidays) | Hatred, aggressive, rage, war, raises blood pressure, fear<br><br>Financial debt—in-the-red<br><br>Embarrassment—red in the face<br><br>Associate with the erotic—red light district<br><br>Associated with communism—red flag | Under red lighting, our body secretes more adrenalin, increasing our blood pressure and our rate of breathing while raising our body temperature just slightly. | Used to increase impulse buying, often used for fast-food restaurants indicating quick, fast service. |
| **PINK** | Mostly positive: feminine, sweet, babyish, delicate, passion (when hue is closer to red) | Physically weakening—use in jail cells or clothing of prison inmates to calm tempers | Pink to soothe upset stomach—Pepto Bismal<br><br>Has been known to heal headaches | Popular color for the cosmetic industry. Color name is often more lavish to increase appeal such as "passion fruit" (Skorinko, Kemmer, et. al, 2006, p. 979). |
| **BLUE** | Associated with water; cool, calm, comfortable, relaxing, clean; successful in bathrooms<br><br>Vary shades to prevent boredom and depressive affect.<br><br>Royalty, coolness, truth, loyalty, success (first place), security, high-technology, nautical, comfort, wetness, cleanliness<br><br>Has been known to reduce the appetite<br><br>*Light-blue:* Gentle, reflective<br><br>*Navy-blue:* Strength, authority (uniformed men and women) | Introversion, sadness, depression, cold, low-class, isolation, loneliness, gloominess<br><br>Blue and bluish-purple are appetite suppressants. | Physiological research shows that blue light will slow your heartbeat, decrease your temperature, and relax your muscles.<br><br>Assists with balance and equilibrium<br><br>Its calming nature has been known to "lower blood pressure, slow pulse rate, or decrease body temperature" (Kopacz, 2004, p. 79). | Fashion consultants recommend wearing blue to job interviews because it symbolizes loyalty. People are more productive in blue rooms. Studies show weightlifters are able to handle heavier weights in blue gyms.<br><br>Lighter shades have been used to symbolize luxury (Tiffany blue). |
| **GREEN** | Relaxed, growth, renewal, eternal life<br><br>Green is the warmest of the cool colors<br><br>Regarded as the most "natural" color<br><br>Excellent color to bring the "outdoors indoors"<br><br>Renewal, freshness, youthful, healthy, tranquility, peaceful, wealthy, may reduce allergic responses and negative reactions to food | Poison, envy, inexperience, immaturity, nausea, sourness, disease, guilt, rawness<br><br>Careful to avoid yellow-green in large quantities—association to sickness, mold, and decay | Assists with balance and equilibrium<br><br>Can ease tremors, twitching, and muscle spasms<br><br>Association of health and well-being | People waiting to appear on TV sit in "green rooms" to relax.<br><br>Hospitals often use green because it relaxes patients.<br><br>Brides in the Middle Ages wore green to symbolize fertility.<br><br>Not a good color for business attire, means immaturity. |

**continued**

**TABLE 2.1** Perceptual Properties and Association of Common Colors (continued)

| HUE | POSITIVE ASSOCIATIONS | NEGATIVE ASSOCIATIONS | HEALTH | CONSUMER BEHAVIOR |
|---|---|---|---|---|
| **YELLOW** | Cheerful, sun, gold, happiness, wisdom, vitality, hope, optimism, and self-esteem<br><br>***Yellow toward blue:*** A yellow ribbon tied around a tree signifies hope and waiting for family members serving in the military to return home.<br><br>***Yellow toward red:*** Intellect, reflection<br><br>***Gold:*** Physical, active, honor, loyal, wealth | Caution, sickness, nervousness<br><br>"Can cause tempers to flare, children to cry, uncontrolled muscular movements in older adults" (Kopacz, 2004, p. 78). | Speeds up the human metabolism<br><br>Was documented by Arab Physician Avicenna as an indicator of liver disorder based on yellowing of skin color (Hope & Walch, 1990, pp. 161–162). | Yellow enhances concentration, hence its use for legal pads and pencils.<br><br><br><br><br>50th wedding anniversary |
| **PURPLE** | Bravery, mystery, royalty, sacred, aristocratic<br><br>***Lavender:*** Spiritual, soft, atmospheric | Conceit, mourning, death, rage, pompous, ostentatious, gloomy | Violet—the color closer to blue than red—has been known to calm anxiety. | Luxury, used to indicate indulgence or expensive items (fine chocolates, automobiles, specialty wines and perfumes). |
| **ORANGE** | Warmth, fruitfulness, brightness, happiness, cheerfulness, jovial, strength, endurance, festivity (holidays)<br><br>When hue is reduced in chroma can be associated with richness and sensuality | Brashness, danger, increases pulse rate, can seem intrusive, inexpensive/cheap | Has been known to increase the amount of oxygen supply to the brain | Associated with inexpensive items and highlight sale items.<br><br>Often used as a color to attract the teens to purchase products (music players, cell phones). |
| **WHITE** | Purity, birth, cleanliness, innocence/virginity, empowerment | Surrender, cowardice, emptiness, clinical | Was documented by Arab Physician Avicenna as an indicator of spleen disorder based on whitening of skin color (Hope & Walch, 1990, pp. 161–162). | Associated with "high-tech" products (Color Wheel Pro).<br><br>Simplicity associated with modern design. |
| **BLACK** | Sophistication and power | Death, emptiness, bad luck | In color therapy it is associated with the kidney and bladder. Can induce sadness, fear, and despair. | In clothing, black can mean safety, security, privacy. |
| **BROWN** | Relates to the comforts of home, wood, and farming<br><br>Relationship to dirt and soil<br><br>Best when combined with hues red, yellow, orange<br><br>Comfort, security, gloom, melancholy, boredom | Men are more likely to say brown is one of their favorite colors.<br><br>Gloom, melancholy, boredom, self-centeredness | No known effects | Associations with chocolate, coffees, espresso, this color has become a color of luxury for merchandise. |
| **GRAY** | Technology, intelligence (gray matter), wealth in association with silver and platinum | confusion, loss of distinction, depression, lack of confidence, old-age | If overly used, may cause depression and loneliness | Known for being a stable color, often use for products to indicate it will have a long useful life (computers, televisions, handheld tech devices, cars). |
| **SILVER** | Elegance, sophistication | No known negative associations | Healing of hormonal imbalances | 25th wedding anniversary<br><br>With the new millennia, silver and platinum overtook gold and brass as the trendier, more popular colors in the home. |

In this chapter, as part of our discussion of the psychology of color perception, we will briefly touch upon how factors of color influence our perception of space and place. Further illustration of each concept within each of the chapters will then connect color and each of the principles of design.

Our visual perception of color can be influenced by (1) the color surrounding the object, (2) the size of the color area (a smaller area of color appears darker, whereas a large area of color appears lighter), (3) the surface characteristics that affect the intensity of a color (rough or smooth texture, gloss and metallic reflection properties), and (4) warm versus cool hues.

Dark colors absorb light and generally make spaces appear smaller. Light colors reflect light and generally make spaces appear larger. Warm colors advance toward the viewer and therefore have the tendency to make spaces seem smaller, whereas cool colors recede visually and therefore expand and make spaces seem

larger. Figure 2.5 illustrates this concept. Student Kelly Geister has selected an original image on the left-hand side, color-keyed the three main hues within the interior space, and identified the color scheme. On the right, she has selected three corresponding hues equal in intensity and color-rendered a new **recoloration** of the space to examine this effect. If there is too much contrast between visual elements, the eye has a difficult time adapting to the changes. This particular exercise is a great tool for refining and improving your illustration, drawing, perspective, and rendering skills.

Yellow is perceived as the brightest of all colors, even over white. Due to this perception, yellow can be an excellent choice for interior spaces where sunlight is at a minimum or in space, such as basements, where natural light may be absent.

A dark-colored piece of furniture against a light background will have more visual weight and sense of stability, as opposed to a light piece of furniture

**FIGURE 2.5** Recoloration using colored pencil and Color-aid papers for an interior space to investigate the perceptual changes between warm and cool colors. (Courtesy of Kelly Geister.)

against a dark background. Rule of thumb: Light objects advance and appear larger; darker objects recede and appear smaller.

The use of values in your color **palette** will add dimension to the space, create visual interest, and elicit positive emotions. The use of pure color without value change or contrast can be overpowering, and in these cases, the color overwhelms the space, resulting in the design elements and details of the space going unnoticed (see Figure 2.6a). This can be successful with enough contrasts of color and pattern, as shown in the living space in Figure 2.6b. Figure 2.6c illustrates acceptable levels of single-hue contrast.

Johannes Itten proposed that perceptions of particular hues can be reinforced abstractly by combining meaning, shape, and form with a particular hue. The formation of all interior design begins with the basic shapes of the square, triangle, and circle, along with their variations—rectangle, rounded triangle, and oval. Itten proposed that the color red, symbolizing power, strength, and stimulation, relates to the square, which, with its horizontal and vertical lines, is associated with the same characteristics. Red, as a powerful color, and the stability of a square combine to increase the perception of "structural planes and sharp angles" (Birren, 1992, p. 171). A triangle relates to yellow, with the angularity of the shape symbolizing a sense of weightlessness; also the color symbol for thought. The color yellow represents the heavens and the sun and is supported by the sides of a triangle slanting upward from the base. Blue relates to the circle for relaxation, motion, and "celestial" qualities (Birren, 1992, p. 171). Orange is for knowledge, creativity, and trust, and is supported by variations of the square—a trapezoid or rectangle. Orange is closely related to red and therefore suggests the same rigid qualities of "angles and details" (Birren, 1992, p. 171). Violet relates

**FIGURE 2.6** (a) Top. Use of a single color overwhelms space, losing focus on the important details. (b) Right. Single hue of vivid blue is successfully balanced with pattern, scale, and contrast. (c) Bottom. Acceptable levels of color contrast. (Top: © Richard Southall/Arcaid/Corbis; right: © Pieter Estersohn/Beateworks/Corbis)

1. light/dark—Excellent contrast   2. dark/light—Acceptable contrast   3. light/light—Poor contrast

**FIGURE 2.7** Right. Color and shape associations.

**FIGURE 2.8** Bottom. Luxury living room in New York City apartment uses strong vertical lines supported by a combination with red hue. (© Getty Images)

to the oval, supporting a spiritual sense, wisdom, mystery, purity, and intuition. And, finally, green relates to the rounded triangle, symbolizing nature, growth, life, and renewal, which one might associate with a tree (Figure 2.7).

In each of these cases, you can make associations with particular elements in our environment. In doing so, you can begin to relate these meanings and characteristics to the interior space. For example, red is known for being aggressive; therefore, strong lines and hard edges would serve to reinforce this concept (Figure 2.8). The same would apply with its application within the interior space by using vertical support columns colored in red or applying the color to a particular strong visual element in your design to suggest strength, importance, or a key design feature. Orange and yellow would follow red with a similar perceived character. Cool colors blue, violet, and green, associated with calm and restfulness, would therefore be supported by applying curvilinear and organic lines (see Figure 2.9). In a spa or space of healing and meditation, blues and greens used with free-form, organic lines support the concept of restfulness. Doubly reinforcing color meanings with design elements and principles strengthens the final design, encouraging meaningful connections between the user and the space.

Colors interact with one another and therefore create visual illusions. In some instances, we may not even realize it is happening. A basic understanding of these perceptual constructs will provide you with the strategies needed to ensure proper color selection for your design projects.

## COLOR CONTRASTS AND OTHER PHENOMENA

Itten identified seven distinct types of color contrast, which designers can use to manipulate the interior space: **simultaneous contrast** (Figure 2.10a), contrast

**FIGURE 2.9** Opposite page. A futuristic bedroom in The Bubble Palace or, *Le Palais Bulles*, is decorated by a contemporary artist in soft blues. It sits on a hillside in Théoule-sur-Mer in the French Riviera, overlooking the Mediterranean Sea. The futuristic mansion, composed of rounded rooms with rotating floors, was designed by Pierre Cardin and architect Antti Lovag. (© Eric Robert/ CORBIS SYGMA)

    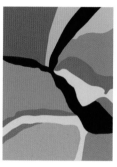  

(a) Simultaneous contrast.  (b) Light/dark contrast.  (c) Cool/warm contrast.  (d) Complementary contrast.  (e) Contrast of hue.  (f) Contrast of saturation or intensity.  (g) Contrast of extension.

**FIGURE 2.10** Seven types of color contrast identified by Itten. (Images courtesy of http://www.worqx.com © Janet Lynn Ford, 1998.)

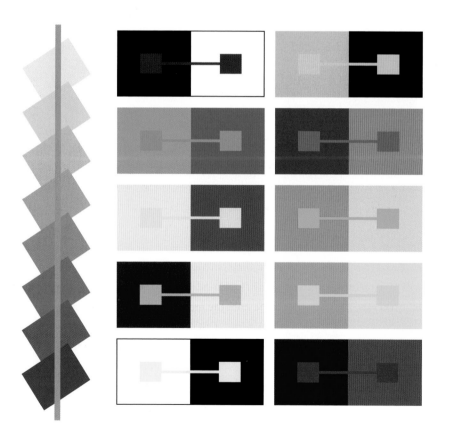

of light/dark (Figure 2.10b), cool/warm contrast (Figure 2.10c), complementary contrast (Figure 2.10d), contrast of hue (Figure 2.10e), contrast of saturation or intensity (Figure 2.10f), and contrast of extension (Figure 2.10g) or the relative quantity or proportion of color. Simultaneous contrast occurs when there is a shift in color from two adjacent hues that have reduced or increased each others' intensity, resulting in a perceived third color. This concept can be seen across the value range illustrated in Figure 2.11. The thin gray bar is the same color; however, as it moves across lighter values, it appears darker, and conversely, when it moves over the darker value, it appears lighter.

Simultaneous contrast results when two equal values create a "vibrancy" effect or strong contrast that occurs around the edges where the two colors meet. This is rarely used in design, and in commercial spaces, it can be a disturbing visual effect. Certain hues will create a more intense vibrancy than other (Figure 2.12). When layering visual elements in a space, be aware of this phenomenon.

**FIGURE 2.11** Left. In this value scale, the thin gray bar is one value; however, as it moves across light to dark values, it is reduced or increased in apparent lightness or darkness, creating a value shift. Right. Examples of simultaneous contrast where a different background results in a perceived difference in hue of the smaller portion of color.

34

FIGURE 2.12 Two colors close in saturation levels can create an afterimage, or vibrancy effect, when placed close to one another. These color combinations are hard to read and visually overstimulating.

FIGURE 2.13 Yellow is the only color that as black is added, shifts to a green shade.

FIGURE 2.14 Bezold effect—change of large color field.

Most hues maintain their original key, shifting only lighter and darker as they move from white to black. Oddly, yellow is the one color that makes a slight chameleon change to green as it moves closer to black. The black neutralizes the red light waves reflected from the yellow object, leaving green to mix with the yellow hue as it draws closer to black (see Figure 2.13).

## Bezold Effect

The **Bezold effect** is common phenomena designers encounter when working with color patterns common with textiles, wall coverings, carpet, or other patterned materials that are available in more than one color palette. Developed by rug maker Wilhelm von Bezold during the nineteenth century, the effect occurs when the largest color area is replaced by a new color, creating a color interaction that changes the overall impression of the design (see Figure 2.14). The same effect can be suc-

cessful if you choose the smaller color field, as long as the contrast and intensity of the newly introduced color is greater than the remaining surrounding hues.

Along the same lines as the Bezold effect, colored patterns seen from afar will optically mix, generating a new hue. For instance, a blue and yellow pattern will mix and produce green. Our eyes are not able to discriminate the individual colors, resulting in the mixture. Complementary colors such as blue and orange will mix and create a muddy tone (Figure 2.15). It is a common error to assume that you can create a color palette from the individual hues within a smaller pattern when the overall colors in the design blend together and create a new color. During the material selection process involving colored patterns, look at the coloration from afar and in the context in which they will be experienced, such as vertically on a wall or horizontally across a piece of furniture, for an accurate representation of the final outcome.

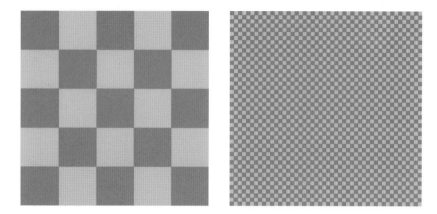

**FIGURE 2.15** Optical mixing of color pattern based on scale and distance of viewer from color source.

## Color Perception Tips and Techniques

The following tips and techniques of color application can be applied to your interior design projects. Experiment with these concepts using study models, manual techniques, or computer rendering to see how the effects may be perceived. Google SketchUp and Adobe Illustrator are excellent computer programs for generating multiple color studies that you can quickly manipulate in order to analyze possible solutions.

- Color has a direct relationship to the physical temperature we perceive and experience in a room. When people are placed into temperature-controlled rooms, one painted a warm hue and the other cool, and are asked to indicate their perceived temperature of the space, participants will indicate the temperature to be slightly higher in the warm-colored space and colder in the cool-colored space (Stone and English, 1998, p. 181). A room that is painted dark colors and receives an adequate amount of natural sunlight has the potential for elevated room temperatures. The dark surfaces will absorb the light energy and then radiate small amounts of heat into the space. This phenomenon can be beneficial to clients by offsetting perceived coolness in colder regions such as Alaska, Minnesota, and Michigan, and in arid regions such as New Mexico, Nevada, or Arizona, where accumulated warmth from daylight harnesses some warmth for cold nights.

- In spaces that are predominately monochromatic (single-hue scheme), applying small amounts of its complement can decrease the monotony and visual boredom.

- Avoid color schemes that use an equal amount of each hue. This can create some confusion, especially when the palette contains more than two colors. The lack of proportion can prevent contrast and emphasis of certain architectural design elements in the space.

## COLOR CONSUMERISM

Color and shape are characteristics of objects designed to attract and retain our attention. Color can be considered as one of the most powerful elements for expressing personality, creating visual appeal, and generating interest in consumer products. Branding and product recognition result from color that communicates information to the consumer, affecting perceptions and preferences, and, ultimately, product sales. Ownership of the product communicates personalization, individuality, identity, meaning, and memories. **Color Marketing Group**, founded in 1962, is nonprofit organization that identifies global color trends in the marketplace. According to this firm, color has the potential to increase a brand's retails sales as much as 80 percent and can be as much as 85 percent of the reason consumers buy a particular product (Color Marketing Group, 2008). Color is important for brand recognition and for eliciting both positive and negative associations with the product. Consumers are no longer content with black and white color choices when purchasing goods. The rise of the millennial generation—young people ages 16 to 25 who have shown an increased need for individualism—has alerted manufactures to create an array of color choices for their products. Apple, Volkswagen, Nike, and cellular phone companies have introduced multiple color options directed specifically toward this age group in an attempt to lure consumers into purchasing their particular brand. According to research conducted by the BuzzBack Market Research and Pantone, Inc., color affected 76 percent of car purchases and 27 percent of personal computers and cellphone purchases in 2005, as well as 86 percent of clothing purchases and 20 percent of personal electronic devices (American Marketing Association, p. 5). In addition, per Color Marketing Group, "Color ads are read up to 42% percent more than similar ads in black & white" (2008, p. 1). These statistics are the direct result of color trends and buying patterns of consumers. Color trends are an excellent way to stay abreast of what consumers are demanding and what is available or to become available in interior-design-related products. As some of you will recall, in earlier days, cell phones were first only available only in black or gray—which are associated with the image of technology and corporate America. In order to attract a larger market, colors were introduced at a later stage. Today, personal technology devices are available in a wide range of colors and patterns, and can be customized to personal preference (Figure 2.16). Observing the retail industry, where many of the products we use for interiors are presented, including custom designs, is an insightful way of staying informed and prepared to select successful colors. Prior to the year 2000, most home interior products were produced in black, white, beige, rusty-browns, and faux finishes. In vogue with the idea of the millennium, the future, and advancing technology, silver began to make its way into the home. Now you can hardly walk into a showroom without chrome, silver, satin-nickel, and pewter finishes abundantly displayed. While often overlooked, identifying the particular consumer products your client likes will enlighten you to potential color preferences. At the least, a good conversation into why the color was chosen and the meaning it may have to the individual is a springboard for ideas.

Finding and selecting colors for a design project can be an overwhelming task. With so many options available in the market, along with influences from TV, magazines, and popular culture tempting you to use current color trends, finding the perfect color might seem all but impossible. Color is a personal choice that should reflect the user. Put simply, if you don't like it, don't use it. If you do not prefer changing colors every one to two years, consider selecting classic color choices and avoid trends.

A color-changing disposable coffee lid from Smart Lid Systems has been awarded a prestigious DuPont® Packaging Award (http://smartlidsystems.com).

The color changes from dark brown to bright red when placed on a hot beverage. This alerts a consumer that a beverage may be too hot. It's also reversible (from red to brown), signaling that a beverage is cooling down.

Technology will trickle down into the home furnishings market and the future of color may include textiles woven with fiber optics, allowing you to change the color of your furnishings with the flip of switch.

## KEY WORDS

Chromo therapy, palette, recoloration, simultaneous contrast, Bezold effect, Color Marketing Group

## LEARNING OUTCOMES

- Demonstrate an understanding of how color relates and changes under varying conditions in interior spaces.
- Know the three key concepts of color perception: (1) color surrounding the object, (2) size of the color area, and (3) surface characteristics affect color (texture, gloss, reflection properties).

FIGURE 2.16 Once an industry of black or gray, now there is no limit to the color array available in cell phones. (Laurence Dutton/Stone/Getty Images)

- Be able to use the seven types of color contrasts in design projects: (1) contrast of hue, (2) light/dark contrast, (3) cool/warm contrast, (4) complementary contrast, (5) simultaneous contrast, (6) contrast of saturation or intensity, and (7) contrast of extension or the relative quantity or proportion of color.

## EXERCISES

The following tools may be used for the following exercises: Color-aid paper, paint samples, or colored artist papers available at your local art supply store, X-acto knife, metal rule, rubber cement, neutral colored (gray works best), and mat board or illustration board for presentation.

1. Select a series of 10 to 15 images from various media in addition to photographing a particular scene that provides you with emotional responses such as: warm/hot, cool/cold, like/dislike, soft/hard, excitement/boredom. If taking photographs, be sure to consider the scene at different times of the day, as light can alter the emotional response. Arrange your images into two organized collages, one for positive emotional response and the other for negative. Analyze why each image elicited your responses. This is a great tool to have for potential clients as a means to begin discussions for color in your design projects.

2. Visit a local retail establishment. Locate several examples of how color is used to market and increase consumers' potential to buy its products. Analyze the way the colors are used, and explain how the design and color may entice the consumer to buy. Pay attention to the age group or type of person the product is targeting and why.

3. The following is an exercise in recoloration:

    a. Select a full-page color photo of an interior space from a design publication.

    b. Using the photograph of an interior space, analyze the color usage and document the major and minor hues used.

    c. Locate these colors within a color aid packet or paint chips from a local paint retailer.

    d. Redraw (tracing/outlining, etc.) the interior using a black pen (felt tip works best). Use drafting equipment when necessary to draw straight vertical/horizontal/diagonal lines.

    e. Rework the room interior with a contrast warm/cool palette by using a different color scheme with balance in chroma and values from the original photo.

    f. Mount the original photograph and the recoloration with your color samples from your color aid packet or paint samples onto a sheet of illustration board. Place your color samples below each photograph.

    g. Label both drawings with their respective color scheme, and provide a comparative analysis of the color transformation to the interior.

4. See Table 2.2 for an exercise to find your color preferences. This is a great tool to use for your future design projects when you need to determine a client's preference for colors.

5. See Table 2.3 for a color perception quiz.

    a. Using color artists papers, Microsoft Word drawing tools, paint programs, or Adobe Illustrator, generate a composition using the Bezold effect. Next, re-create the same design replacing one of the key colors from the original with a new color that results in the Bezold effect.

**TABLE 2.2** Color Preferences Revealed

| STEP 1 | 1. Think of a color, any color that immediately pops into your head. It does not have to be your favorite or least favorite, just the first color that comes to mind. |
|---|---|
| | 2. If you could move to any location in the world, where would it be? List two to four colors you associate with this place. |
| | 3. As a child, we all have favorite rooms, whether our own or places we've played. When you were between the ages of 5 and 9; what was your favorite room in the home? Now list the colors you remember seeing in this space. How did they make you feel? Were the colors chosen and the rooms designed to make you feel a certain way? |
| | 4. Think of your favorite vacation you've taken in the past. List two to three colors you see in this place. Write about their special properties and how they made the place memorable and enjoyable. |
| | 5. Think of a person who has had a significant impact in your life. What color(s) do you associate with that person? Why? |
| | 6. Now, open your bedroom closet door and peer inside. Do certain colors dominate your wardrobe? If so, list three of them. |
| | 7. Gifts or cherished memorabilia often leave us with positive feelings, remind us of a loved one, a place visited, or a time of joy in one's life. Think of the most cherished object in your home; the one thing you would grab if your house was about to disappear. What color is it? |
| | 8. Consider an event in your life that might have made you sad or angry. Do you see one or two colors that reflect that memory? |
| STEP 2 | Look at the colors you have written and list the top two to three that occur most often. These are the colors you're most likely to feel comfortable around. Examine those colors listed from question 8. These are possibly colors you may feel uncomfortable around. |

(Adapted from McCleary, 2002, p. 7)

**TABLE 2.3** Color Perceptions Quiz

| Which color relaxes the nervous system? | RED spaces would make someone feel anxious, but rooms with red accents make people lose track of time. Bars and casinos often use this color to get people to 'stick around.' |
|---|---|
| Which color makes people feel anxious? | PINK If you are in a pink room, you just don't have enough energy to get angry! Pink has been used for criminal uniforms and wall surfaces of penitentiary to eliminate conflict amount cellmates. |
| Which color has the potential to make people angry? | ORANGE Early man learned to keep away from foods that were blue, purple, or black, for they would normally be poisonous. Preference towards this color for food due to pleasant flavors associated with oranges, mangoes, apricots, pumpkins, and other yellow and yellow-orange vegetables. |
| Which color can cause fatigue and lack of energy? | BLUE causes your body to produce chemicals that calm the nervous system. |
| Which color is known to make people nervous or tense? | BLACK creates a sense of endlessness and is a "color" that does not get brighter during the day. Also associated with night, witchcraft, and death. Bad luck for a black cat to cross your path. |
| Which color is considered one of the most appetizing? | YELLOW Highly luminescent, pure yellow can hurt the eyes and causes people to lose their tempers more easily. |

color + balance

## 3

Just as graphic designers manage visual information on a page, interior designers manage visual information within our immediate surroundings. We use balance to make sense of the world around us—to make our environments aesthetically pleasing. To achieve balance, we strive to create order among chaos for the purpose of organizing our living spaces. This order serves to communicate to others the design intent. When color is used with the design principles—for instance, balance—unity within a space can occur.

## WHAT IS BALANCE?

**Balance** refers to the relationship of different hues to one another when each is perceived to be equal in perceived visual weight. We have a natural attraction to beauty and images pleasing to the eye. Take the human body, for instance. Greek artisans have portrayed the beauty of the human body in art and sculpture for centuries. The symmetry of the human form represents pure aesthetic beauty that has been emulated in historical and contemporary architecture and interior design. Research indicates a preference for symmetry. People are more attracted to objects that contain symmetry—a perfect balance of parts (Lidwell, Holden, Butler, 2003, pp. 190–191).

When speaking of balance and design, we must first make a distinction between physical balance and perceived or visual balance. Physical balance is the optimal measure of gravitational forces that keeps you from falling. Like a scale, it is the distribution of weight to achieve equilibrium. This type of balance is separate from the type of balance we manipulate in our visual fields to achieve an aesthetically pleasing painting, photograph, landscape, building, or interior. Perceptual balance involves the object itself (size, scale) and the visual weight of the color (appears heavy or light). The amount of color used, the number of different colors used, the visual weight of the colors, and the locations of the colors within the space are the four key factors in establishing good color balance.

Balance is a general term used to describe the physical or perceptual state of equality or order of objects within a larger composition. Balance is described by three types: symmetry (formal balance), asymmetry (informal balance), and radial balance (radiating from a central axis). Symmetry is the most common type of balance used in architecture and interior design. Symmetry ("measured together") comes from the Latin word *symmetria* and the Greek word *symmetros*. **Symmetry** (formal balance) is the arrangement of elements on either side of an implied axis that are equally balanced and of the same shape and form (i.e., mirror image). When symmetry is achieved, a state of beauty and balance occurs. Balance out of chaos creates order; order creates purpose and meaning within our physical environment. Chaos results when there is no relation to or consideration of the design elements that make up our physical environment. Symmetry is everywhere around us. Examine the petals of a flower, a seashell, an artichoke, a pinecone, a snowflake, the human body, and even animals.

**Radial** balance is achieved by the equal rotation of design elements around a central axis. This is the least of the three balance types to impact color planning and is more of an organizational concept. Radial balance could be applied to a situation where one color is used as a focal point within a space where neutrals are predominant. In this instance, the colored focal point would be centrally located and all other design elements would extend outward (see Figure 3.1).

Balance is an important part of the design process. Without balance, the remaining principles and elements get lost and a lack of cohesion in the finished design results. Balance is considered the most important and is often listed first among the principles of design. Without balance, chaos ensues and has the potential to elicit a negative reaction to interior spaces and often compels the user to "solve the problem" by fixing, in some cases, what they do not know to be wrong until balance is achieved. We have become so accustomed to living with balance that we sometimes take the phenomenon for granted. It is only when it is removed that we become aware that something is awry. Balance is the yin and yang of our visual experience. The contrast between order and chaos sends the message to our brain that something does not feel right. This can be a daunting task in the field of interior design, more so for the inexperienced home or business owner or for a student studying design. To pair the property of balance with color, one must cultivate proper skills and basic understanding of their underlying influences within our physical environments.

## WHAT IS *COLOR* BALANCE?

Balance is the striving to achieve the point of equilibrium between two or more forces. Balance is a means whereby harmony, peace, and connection can be made between the observer and that which is observed. This visual process is innately intuitive; however, a series of steps can be used to ensure a finished interior space that incorporates a balance of colors.

The spatial context of the color used can vary depending on the size of the space, lighting both natural and artificial, influences from and interaction with other colors, textures, and the physical orientation of the architectural space (vertical walls or horizontal floors, or angles and arcs in limitless combinations).

The addition or subtraction of color in the interior space will correctly convey the impression or perception the designer intends. This balance does not represent a physical weight of color, rather the perceptual attributes one assigns to each particular color: If you examine each of the primary and secondary colors in the next section, you can assign a numeric order from 1 to 6, 1 being the lightest and 6 being the heaviest for each of these primary and secondary hues. If this is expanded to include the tertiary colors, the balance scale extends further. Note that these colors are being represented in their purist sense, not influenced by adding white (tint) or black (value) to the color.

Interiors, at a minimum, should attempt to contain a three-value scheme. This allows a space to maintain depth and visual interest. Interiors that are too light appear delicate and almost unnatural, potentially lacking any interest. Mid tones can become too complacent and uninteresting, and an interior with the dark values only can be overwhelming and depressing. Too little or too much of any one color can lead to an interior that is disengaging, is lacking unity, and can be perceived as chaotic. Balance is most critical in establishing harmony and unity within an interior. We will discuss harmony and unity in a later chapter.

When clients ask "what colors should I use?" or "what colors are trendy?" my goal is to redirect them, establishing the rule that no one color is good or bad. Rather, it is how the color is used within the space that determines its success in addition to the design style being established in the interior with direct relation to the architecture of the building. The first task is to determine what colors

**FIGURE 3.1** Mid-century modern living space using radial balance as a design tool in the architecture, interior furnishings, and accessories, with natural colors extending the space and reflecting the flora and fauna beyond. (© Alan Weintraub/Arcaid/Corbis)

appeal to you. An interior that is designed with palettes chosen by the designer or by recommendation of the latest fashion magazine could end up feeling like a space that is disconnected from its inhabitants.

Our brains want to "connect the dots." When a space lacks good color balance, a disconnection of the space's components emerges. If only a portion of the "dots" are connected, then only a portion of the design will be aesthetically pleasing and enjoyable.

## TYPES OF COLOR BALANCE

"Balance enforces the demand for oppositional groups . . . and it achieves its objectives as soon as oppositional forces are clearly identified" (Ellinger, 1980, p. 28). In order to achieve this, we must have contrast of hues, values, and chroma. In this chapter we discuss four types of balance that can be achieved through color application: value contrast (light/dark), hue balance (complements), intensity contrast (bright/dull), and size of color area (large/small).

### Value Contrast (Light/Dark)

**Contrast** is opposition in order to show or emphasize differences between two objects. When working with color, adequate contrast creates more stimulating

results. The amounts of contrast desired depend the space types and the design application needed. High contrast should be used for areas where safety is a concern, such as on edges to differentiate between changes in level to avoid falls, or low contrast, such as a medical waiting room, where limiting anxiety or tension is critical. In each of these examples, the contrast of light and dark surroundings is the key.

With regard to visual weight, the lightness or darkness of a color refers to the perceived color weight of an object. In this instance, we are not concerned about the physical weight or heaviness, rather the weight imparted by our perceptions of the color itself. White is perceived as lighter than black. A black object will appear to be visually heavier than white (Figure 3.2). The Munsell value scale illustrates a nine-step scale, from pure black (1) to pure gray, which is an equal mixture of black and white (5), to pure white (9). See Figure 3.3. This illustrates a scale that proceeds from heavy to light. Now, let's utilize this same scale to organize our primary and secondary hues—red, blue, yellow and violet, green, orange. Yellow is perceived as being the brightest or lightest of the primary and secondary hues, whereas blue is perceived as the darkest. Based on the apparent lightness or darkness, we can assign a range from heavy to light with any hue. Note that when working with multiple colors, the physical comparison between those colors will

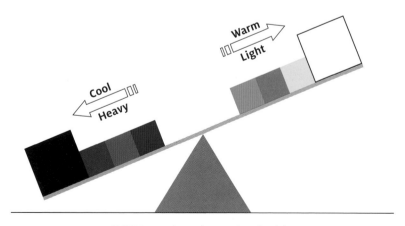

FIGURE 3.2 Value and perception of weight.

result in the "weight scale" for that particular color palette. Let's take yellow for an example. Yellow can assume the role of the heaviest hue in your palette when grouped with lighter values of a darker color, such as a soft, pale pastel or a hue tinted or toned with white or gray (Figure 3.4). In this example we purposefully assign dominance to yellow in our color scheme by downplaying the lightness and chroma of the supporting hues. Since we typically work with samples of dyed material or paint swatches, you will want to practice recognizing when a physical material sample's hue represents a tint (adding white), tone (adding gray), or shade (adding black) of color. With value contrast, the relative lightness or darkness of any neutral (black, white, gray) or hues (red, blue, yellow) when compared to one another results in the "weight scale" for that particular project.

The second type of value contrast results not from comparing two individual colors side by side, but rather by comparing them when they share the same area or overlapping within a visual field. Generally speaking, a dark color on a light background will appear to be much darker than it really is. Conversely, a light color on a dark background will appear lighter than it really is. This manipulation discovered by Josef Albers is explained further in his book *Interaction of Color*. This principle, often referred to as "one color like two," illustrates the juxtaposition of colored elements in a space. The vertical and horizontal planes of our living spaces (wall and floors) serve as backdrops to the objects we place within them. Being that these are the largest spans of surface within our spaces, they are likely to contain the largest color area. Therefore, depending on the color that is placed in relation to those areas, it can now appear lighter or darker. Color should be organized within the interior to draw a logical color order to the visual information.

Figure 3.5a illustrates a modern bedroom space. The interior lacks color or contrast, with the exception of the silver-colored seating, to distinguish key visual elements, such as the bedroom area from the sitting area. Additionally, the left side of the space contains more visual information: a cabinet, two chairs, and table that generate the perception of heaviness versus the right side, which appears lighter in weight. In Figure 3.5b the addition of wood grain on the cabinet adds texture and interest, and the assigned darker, muted color scheme on

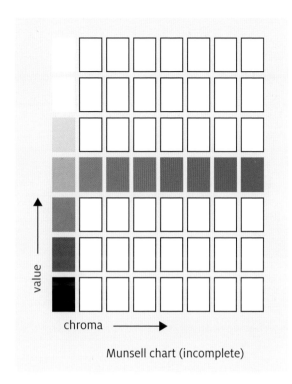

**FIGURE 3.3** Munsell value and chroma scale.

**FIGURE 3.4** Yellow, perceived as being the lightest in visual weight of the primary and secondary colors, can become the heaviest when balanced with lighter or pastel hues.

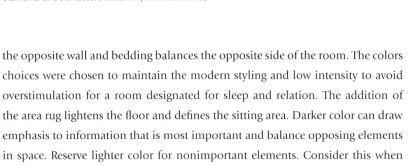

**FIGURE 3.5a** Modern bedroom space lacking visual color contrast and balance of design elements and surfaces. (Illustration by Steven Stankiewicz)

**FIGURE 3.5b** Introduction of blues and blue-green, texture, and value contrast add visual interest and balance to the interior. (Illustration by Steven Stankiewicz)

the opposite wall and bedding balances the opposite side of the room. The colors choices were chosen to maintain the modern styling and low intensity to avoid overstimulation for a room designated for sleep and relation. The addition of the area rug lightens the floor and defines the sitting area. Darker color can draw emphasis to information that is most important and balance opposing elements in space. Reserve lighter color for nonimportant elements. Consider this when choosing your palette.

## Hue Balance (Complements)

Complementary colors are those colors that when placed next to one another intensify the other hue, making each to appear brighter. These colors are directly opposite each other on a color wheel. See Figure 3.6. The phenomenon occurs due to the lack of relation between the two. This creates a very strong contrast and in turn creates asymmetrical balance of light/bright and dark/dull depending on the property of that particular color, as previously illustrated by the arrangement of primary and secondary hue by visual weight. **Asymmetry** (or informal balance) results when elements on either side of an implied axis are equal in color weight but vary in shape and size. This is often more visually interesting and can be achieved through value and/or hue contrast (Figure 3.7).

The colors provide to each other what they lack in themselves. Green complements red, since red contains no traces of the hue green. Orange complements blue, and yellow complements violet for the same reasons. By bringing the two contrasting colors together, a harmonic order of color is achieved and balance ensues.

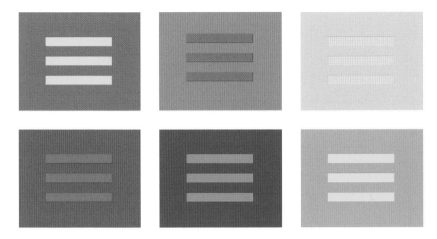

FIGURE 3.6 Asymmetrical balance through complementary contrast.

The palette in Figure 3.8 is composed of the warm hues of red-orange and yellow-orange; yellow can be balanced with the introduction of a cool hue (blue-green) to add visual contrast and balance the bright and dull hues. When used in different proportions, this color combination, will balance the palette, resulting in a more pleasing aesthetic, as shown in Figure 3.9. Introducing the blue cools the warm palette, making it more palatable for an interior space.

## Intensity Contrast (Bright/Dull)

The relative brightness or dullness of color is established by adding the complementary color to a particular hue or with the addition of gray. Color intensity does not refer to *lightness* or *darkness*—that occurs from adding white (light) or black (dark) to a color.

Purity of hue, or chroma, results when a color is not influenced by other colors. Red in its purist form contains no traces of white, black, gray, or other color. However, once gray is added to the pure hue red, the intensity or brightness of the color begins to decrease. A brighter color will advance, whereas a duller color will recede. Adding pure white produces a tint (pink), and adding pure black pro-

FIGURE 3.7 Asymmetrical balance. The two different shapes and sizes are made to appear that they have the same visual weight by assigning the perceived lighter hue (green) to the larger square shape to balance the smaller darker circle in violet.

duces a shade (burgundy). The same perceptual properties of weight will apply with light colors and dark colors, known as value. Light colors will appear to advance toward the viewer, and dark colors will tend to recede. Intensity changes in color become more apparent as the color strays from its original hue more toward gray. The property of advancing and receding correlates to the apparent visual weight of the colors as well. Light colors will appear closer and visually light; darker colors will appear farther away and visually heavier.

Figure 3.10 illustrate the differences between light, dark, and dull colors. Notice which colors appear closer and farther away in addition to the perception of visual weight where the colors appear lighter and heavier. Interior spaces are generally more accepted and pleasing to the user when small amounts of intense color are balanced by larger amounts of duller color. Variations in intensity do

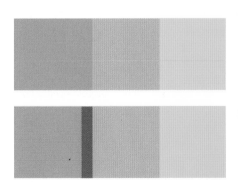

FIGURE 3.8 Palette of warm hues requires the addition of a cool hue (blue-green) to balance the intensity level.

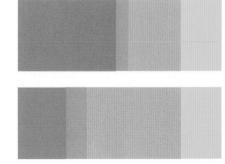

FIGURE 3.9 Color balance corrected with addition of contrasting hue in two intensity levels.

Pure hue blue      Tint of blue      Shade of blue      Dull (chroma intensity)

**FIGURE 3.10** Top. Weight shifts with value and intensity of a single hue.

**FIGURE 3.11** Bottom. Modern dining space with red accents. (© Dan Forer/Beateworks/Corbis)

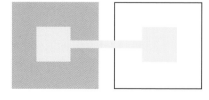

not change the original hue. Assign darker, heavier colors toward the bottom one-third of space and work upward to light values of your palette. Reversing this order is unsettling and is contrary to the natural gravitational pull. However, this technique can be reversed in spaces of large volume to visually lower ceiling height. Using a darker color on the ceiling and floors will lessen the apparent vertical height, compressing the perceived volume (Figure 3.11).

## Size of Color Area (Large/Small)

The larger the amount of color used, the lighter it will appears; the smaller the amount of color used, the darker it appears. This effect is intensified in colors that are placed against a secondary color of opposite lightness or darkness. **Color interaction** involves the contrast of light and dark values; when one value is placed next to or surrounded by the other, the visual weight of the smaller of the two color areas is intensified. When using this contrast, you must consider not only the weight of the color that is changing but also the hue itself, depending

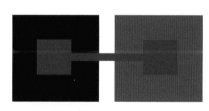 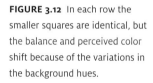

**FIGURE 3.12** In each row the smaller squares are identical, but the balance and perceived color shift because of the variations in the background hues.

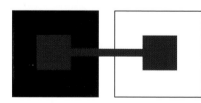

on the background color. In Figure 3.12 two equally weighted background colors are used, one belonging closer to the blue family and one to the red. At the center of each square is a smaller square of hue consisting of a combination of the two background colors—in this case a red-violet. The background color of each square is visually subtracted from the smaller square, and the result is the appearance of two completely different hues resulting in value shift or "weight" change. The smaller square appears redder on the left side, whereas the smaller square on the right side appears bluer. The remaining two images represent additional shifts in color balance relative to the background colors influence on their perceived weight. This phenomenon in balance shift, known as simultaneous contrast, was discussed in Chapter 2.

During your color selection process, determine which of your hues, based on the information presented, is likely to consume more of the visual space. Organize your colors by weight, and assign their location to maximize your effect of increased or decrease volume. You do not want all your hues to appeal equally balanced in light/dark or bright/dull. This will lead to a drab, lifeless interior. Later in the text we will discuss proportion. Accomplished color schemes are the result of the color balance techniques and proper portioning of each hue.

## LOCATION OF A COLOR PALETTE WITHIN THE 3-D ENVIRONMENT

The location of colors within the physical environment is just as important to a balanced composition as the selection of color itself. The shape of interior space is divided into specific surface planes: vertical surfaces (walls) and horizontal surfaces (wall, floors, and ceiling). Our eyes would otherwise move around a space randomly, but color acts as a carrier, focusing our attention on specific design features and elements and repeating the color to guide your observation throughout the

**FIGURE 3.13** (a) Top. The color balance is shifted too heavily to the warm side of the color wheel, creating an uncomfortable, hot, retail experience. (b) Bottom. Introduction of cool hue softens the warm palette, providing contrast between surfaces and a more palatable experience.

(Illustrations by Steven Stankiewicz)

# color + balance

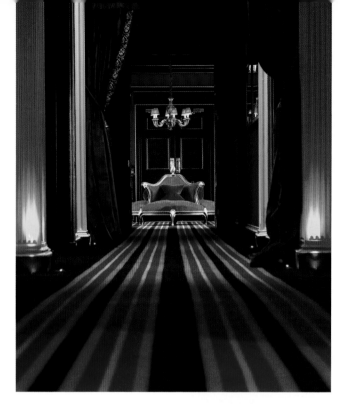

**FIGURE 3.14**(a) Left. Prestonfield Hotel, Edinburgh, Scotland. A combination of high and low light levels, strong vibrant reds, and bold stripes emphasizes the hotel corridor leading guests to the round sofa in the lounge area. (© Adrian Houston/Loop Images/Corbis)

**FIGURE 3.14**(b) Right. White crown molding set two-thirds up the wall contrasts with the taupe walls, creating the illusion of decreased ceiling height and a more intimate interior. (© Look Photography/Beateworks/Corbis)

**FIGURE 3.15** Above. Hasbro office break room uses teal and purple to embody the childlike qualities for which the company is known. Diagonal-patterned flooring adds to the fun atmosphere offset with the room's natural geometry. (© Adrian Wilson/Beateworks/Corbis)

50

space. Color can connect the design elements and create a sense of harmony within the space. A lack of "color connection" leaves the viewer attempting to "connect the dots," trying to find a logical sense in the visual arrangement of elements.

In the retail space in Figure 3.13a, the color palette can be perceived as hot and uncomfortable. This imbalance can be offset by reducing the intensity of the red or the introduction of a cooler hue, green (Figure 3.13b). Be careful to avoid having a color palette that is "a combination of half warm and half cool," as this will only send an "unclear message" to the users to the intended experience—warm or cool (Eiseman, 1998, p. 154). Chapter 6 presents proportional strategies to avoid such an occurrence.

## Illusion of Vertical and Horizontal Space

We can define our living spaces into two general experiences, the vertical and horizontal `experience. Our floor and ceiling serve as our horizontal planes and the walls our vertical planes. Balance can be achieved and maintained by location of the color choices onto these planes. Isolating color onto one plane alone can visually slice the spaces into segments and thus create visual imbalance. Contrasting lines of color can be an effective way to create illusions that reduce over- and under-exaggerated spatial size, balancing the user experience.

Stripe flooring running the length of an interior (Figure 3.14a) as well as crown molding running the width (Figure 3.14b) could be used interchangeably to increase the apparent depth, width, and scale of a space. Spatial extremes can be modified in this manner to adjust visually unbalanced interiors. In the second figure, the higher contrast increases this effect. Running colored lines in a slight diagonal to the vertical planes in a space can create the illusion of more depth (Figure 3.15). In this example, the smaller, tighter spacing of colored lines is more effective than a larger spacing. This tool is successful in smaller confined areas and adds more interest to simple interiors. In large-volume spaces, this technique can be used vertically to balance the volume and bring space to a more comfortable human scale (Figure 3.16). In Figure 3.17 contrasting blue and white stripes and check pattern decreases the spatial volume but increases the perception of depth.

**FIGURE 3.16** Residential entrance foyer. (© Michel Arnaud/Beateworks/Corbis)

**FIGURE 3.17** Opposite page. Interior Togoville Cathedral, Togo, West Africa.

(© Atlantide Phototravel/Corbis)

## Chroma/Value Factor

Another common error in color usage relates to the application and variation of value and chroma within an interior space. Too much variation of chroma (high intensity not balanced with dull) or value (light not balanced with dark) creates little contrast, an element essential to an interior that provides a visually pleasing space through balance of opposing forces. A level of contrast must be present. See Figure 3.18 for examples of poor color contrasts (too light, too dark); the bottom palette successfully balances both. A certain amount of dark is needed for the eyes to rest. Without the darker areas, eye strain could occur for the intense lighter and brighter hues that will reflect more natural light into the eyes—similar to the experience of walking from inside a building to the bright outdoors. Consider this especially in spaces with a large percentage of intense color. Intense color should always be balanced with dull color or neutral white, black, or gray to avoid eye strain from constant shifts in values.

This error typically falls in conjunction with a lack of relation between the level of brightness and dullness of a color. For example, the colors shown in Figure 3.19 (top) illustrate two complementary colors, red and green, whose intensity has been grayed to a duller version of their original selves. In stark contrast, the same colors red and green are shown in Figure 3.19 (middle), although there is an obvious lack of balance due to the intensity level. The green is too intense and appears unrelated to the red despite their being complementary colors. Figure 3.19 (bottom) illustrates the green corrected by muting the hue to balance the red.

## Single-Color Overload

A color palette is not confined to any number of required hues within one space. As a general rule of thumb, rooms can contain as little as one color and should contain no more than five colors. With color schemes consisting of more than

Palette balance is weak, not stimulating.

Palette balance is too dark, not stimulating.

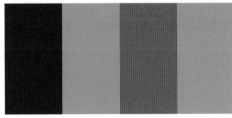

Palette balances light and dark value adding interest.

**FIGURE 3.18** Color palettes with weak contrast and corrected palette integrating both lights and darks.

Balanced value and intensity of complementary hues.

Incorrect intensity balance with new red hue.

Correct intensity balance with new red hue.

**FIGURE 3.19**

**FIGURE 3.20** Monochromatic palette with no balance of light and dark values. The addition of lighter values corrects color balance in the bottom image.

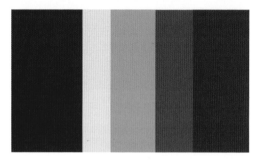

## Multiple-Color Overload

When considering four or more colors within an interior space, care has to be taken to ensure the colors relate to one another. Remember, to create balance within any space, pleasing relationships must be present. Apparent relationships help the person living in or using the space to make personal and functional connections, promoting comprehension of what is being viewed. Otherwise, disorientation may result when the user first experiences a place. When you consider large commercial spaces, such as hospitals, retail establishments, or large office buildings, color chaos could make wayfinding almost impossible. If too many separate colors are chosen, the space will appear unbalanced, with little connection among the elements.

The way we decide to dress directly relates to balancing and making sound color choices. Imagine for a moment you decide to dress yourself in blue pants, a green jacket, orange scarf, purple belt, and, for fun, yellow shoes. Would you be comfortable stepping out in public in this color combination? The same rules apply to design; too much color is an overload and creates disorder (Figure 3.21).

## KEY WORDS

Balance, symmetry, radial, contrast, asymmetry, color interaction

## LEARNING OUTCOMES

The following checklist can be used to ensure the key components of color balance are incorporated into your design projects.

* How many different colors are going to be used?
* Have I organized my palette according to their respective visual weights?
* Have I established a balance of light and darkest color in my palette? If not, then readjusting the lightest/darkness of the corresponding colors will be needed.
* Have I assigned the color selections throughout the space, establishing good color balance?
* Have I selected a dominant color for my palette?

fours colors, the first three might be of different hues, with the remaining two a tint or shade of the one or more of the other three. A space that contains only one hue has the potential to become monotonous and boring. To correct this problem, incorporate a variety of contrasts to add visual stimulation within the interior space. One color needs to play the dominant role in your color scheme, with lighter and mid tones balancing the palette. Figure 3.20 illustrates two color palettes, each involving the single hue violet. The top example illustrates too much monotony and no balance of light and dark. The second palette corrects this problem with added value contrast to provide visual stimulation. Notice the darker value is now less dominant and the lighter/brighter values balance the darker values for added contrast. In summary, light colors need to be balanced with dark colors, highly saturated colors need to be balanced with dull colors, and the intensity of colors must relate to one another to create a harmonious palette.

**FIGURE 3.21** Multicolor overload. (Red Cover)

## EXERCISES

1.  a. Construct a value scale and chroma scale using colored paper—that is, the Color-aid® system of colored paper. The exercise will reinforce learning the subtle changes in value and the color terminology (tint, tone, and shade), in addition to recognizing visual color weight.

    b. Select 30 different-colored papers—10 tints, 10 shades, and 10 hues—with less saturated chroma. Organize these hues into three weight scales from lightest to heaviest. This exercise reinforces analyzing color for visual weight while learning to recognize and select color based on these three properties.

2. Create balanced compositions that explore visual weight changes by using background hues of simultaneous contrasts to make "one color like two" and two colors like one. Focus these exercises using single hues of light and dark values versus additional hues that are formed by color mixing. Provide a written analysis of your processes (both successful and not successful attempts) and why the final solution was chosen.

color + rhythm

**FIGURE 4.1**

Top. Nautilus sea-shell. Right. Spiral staircase, Vatican Museum, Rome.

(Top: © Ted Horowitz/ Alamy; right: © Renee Morris/Alamy)

Rhythm is movement. **Rhythm** is a natural evolutionary trait in nature that can be transferred to interior spaces and can be further emphasized with color (Figure 4.1). Alternating hues, progressive values, or contrast of saturation are methods whereby a designer can manipulate interior elements to bring a better rhythmic order to space. Matthew Frederick expresses our movement in space in this way: "The shapes and qualities of architectural spaces greatly influence human experience and behavior, for we inhabit the spaces of our built environment and not the solid walls, roof, and columns that shape it. Positive spaces are almost always preferred by people for lingering and social interaction. Negative space tends to promote movement rather than dwelling in space." (2007, p. 6)

This interplay of solid and void, or contrast, is a methodology that can relate to color usage and therefore be used to create interplay of light and dark for rhythmic harmony. In Figure 4.2 the relationship of light and dark values creates an undulating pattern that ripples from painted color at the distance wall onto the adjoining surface as a textile. The use of a single hue—orange—suggests a focal point in stark contrast to the remaining interior palette of achromatic values, reinforcing the playful character of this color rhythm. Rhythm is the repetition, recurrence, or sequencing of similar design elements in the built environment, creating a pattern. Rhythm can also be achieved through color contrast or similarity in hue, value, and intensity. The hierarchy we assign to architectural elements with color helps to communicate the activity for a particular space, assists **wayfinding** (physical awareness if one's place or orientation) in a space, and adds priority or focus. The rhythm of color guides us like a map to understand the functionality of the space and to create a holistic experience. Arnheim is noted in *The Interior Dimension* as saying that "if humans are to interact with a building functionally there must be visual continuity" (Malnar & Vodvarka, 1992, p. 73). Good continuity of space occurs when the users have an ongoing visual experience of the space. As a person moves through a space, the use of color and rhythm should guide him or her along the path or intended sequence. There is no beginning or end to a design unless there is the desire for the user to stop and pause to experience items of importance. In this case, you may apply focal points or points of interests such as a sculpture or a directory to aid in orienting users to their position in the interior.

## COLOR AND MUSIC

In much the same way composers score crescendos and triumphant noise balanced with soft repose (contrasts or accents) in smooth flowing melodies, where one note combined with many creates chords, one color combined with many creates visual harmony. In the late nineteenth and early twentieth centuries, theorists began to make psychological associations between color and music. Goethe noted the work of J. L. Hoffman, who proposed musical timbre created by instruments related to certain colors: "yellow for clarinets, red for trumpet, crimson for flutes, ultramarine for violins, and so on" (Gage, 1993, p. 236). The high pitch of the trumpet and flute clearly suggest the strength and brightness of red, whereas soft, melodic pitch of the violin suggests blues. This example illustrates that, universally, aspects of color are not so far removed for other activities. When we can draw the connections and make analogies, the once-overwhelming use of color can become easier for the aesthetician. As with musical compositions, color can be used to create rhythm and movement. Placement of hues in rhythmic succession helps to unify pieces of visual information in space. Whether your color is moving vertically, horizontally, or diagonally, it can be used to maximize the visual impact required for your project. The horizontal line created and contrasted with surroundings by the gray metallic finish in Maggie's Cancer Centre in Figure 4.3 orients you toward the entrance location with a dynamic wall detail. Contrasting the material with the background and floor surface emphasizes the form and movement we experience.

## NATURE AND RHYTHM

Interior designers and architects seek inspiration from many sources. From the jagged lines of mountaintops to the simple curves of a calla lily, organic patterns from nature are all around us. Simple organic forms have influenced the work of designers Verner Panton, Karim Rashid, and Philippe Starck. We draw inspiration and examples from nature into interior designs, from simple chairs to ornate light fixtures, using recognizable forms that allow the human being to immediately form a connection with the object or interior space being experienced. Circular repetitive forms of a shell, the angles and rhythms of a palm frond, or the radial symmetry in the petals of a flower are examples of natural pattern forms.

**FIGURE 4.2** Bedroom with striped drapery and mural carries the eye around the space at The Standard Hotel, Los Angeles. (© Tim Street-Porter/Beateworks/Corbis)

**FIGURE 4.3**
Maggie's Cancer Centre, Inverness, Scotland. Designed by Page & Park.
(© VIEW Pictures Ltd/Alamy)

(a) Contemporary restaurant with wood panel walls and ceiling and organic shapes. (© Tim Street-Porter/Beateworks/Corbis)

(b) Pecten jacobaeus shell.
(© Radius Images/Corbis)

**FIGURE 4.4** Bio-inspired colors, patterns, and textures.

(c) Spiral Pendant by Verner Panton, 1969. (© Corbis. All Rights Reserved.)

(d) School of sardines. (Jens Kuhfs/Photographer's Choice/Getty)

These patterns exist in every natural form whether human, animal, or plant. Richard Dubé states that "when a designer chooses a pattern form on the basis of aesthetics, the choice will likely be driven by one or more of the following factors: emotions, scale, texture, or broad applicability" (1997, p. 63).

The Baháʼí Temple in New Delhi is a pure geometric form that represents a giant lotus flower. This symbol represents the spiritual connection the lotus flower has to the Baháʼí faith. The light color reflects the white of the flower, and the use of natural progression of shape and size adds rhythmic order to the architecture. Nature and color, therefore, can be a metaphor. Using **bio-inspired** color and design creates a personal connection, familiarity, and relevance to an object or space that may not have existed otherwise.

Nature provides inspiration for interior designers. A designer (or the manufacturers of paint and textiles he or she chooses) might try to replicate the exact "Leaf Green" or "Sunset Orange" that can be seen in the outdoors. The architectural column was inspired by palm trees. Ceilings radiating outward from a focal center emulate the many concentric circles found in nature—a rippling pond, a conch shell, a bird's nest, and more. Familiar patterns in interior design obviously imitate nature: paisleys, floras, spirals, and anything that grows from the ground and appears to blossom. Many ceilings are designed to emulate the sky, offering an open and airy feel to the users of the space. A den is more likely to resemble a cave, with highly textured wood and darker colors. This imparts a cocooned feeling to the user and is most often associated with residential interiors or libraries. Think of the many instances where interior designers have simulated ground cover with creative floor coverings and day or night skies with innovative ceilings—with the shape of the ceiling itself or the color it is dressed in. The honeycomb, the snowflake, the butterfly wing, and many more organic materials feed the imaginations of designers. As a beginning interior designer, you should collect photos and actual samples from nature that give you a positive response and work these patterns and color schemes into your designs. More advanced challenges might incorporate fractal geometry, the DNA double helix, or something visible under a microscope. The possibilities are endless. The goal is to tap into nature and create something man-made that pleases the user for a long time.

The ocean is an excellent source for beautiful colors, textures, and patterns to influence and inspire your designs. The interior of the contemporary restaurant in Figure 4.4a illustrates a color palette of warm browns and beige, curvilinear ceiling design, and repetition of a striped pattern reminiscent of a seashell (Figure 4.4b). The spiral pendant by Verner Panton, from 1970, is made of chrome-plated plastic suspended by clear nylon strings (Figure 4.4c). The floating and spiraling effect reminds you of a swimming school of silver colored sardines (Figure 4.4d). Any other colored finish would not be successful with the intended design outcomes of this light fixture.

Student Julee Owens developed a convertible seating group—"The Klatch"—inspired by the coloration of the yellow-jacket wasp and its nest (Figure 4.5). Selected materials coloration, pattern, shape, and form work to emulate the natural forms and, in turn, create a unique, functional, and versatile product for interior use.

Noticing color and rhythm in nature can provided an extended source of inspiration for your interior design projects. See Figures 4.6a to 4.6g for examples of color in nature and color rhythm expressed through the progression of colors on the natural forms.

Recognizing the natural patterns provides an additional source for mimicking shapes and patterns that can be used in your designs. These palettes have been prepared in proportional relationship relative to the natural form. The proportions indicate the "natural" progression of color nature can provide you. Being observant of your surrounding will open up a wide range of color patterns in nature and will be an effective tool to help you plan your proportional relationships of color in your space plans.

## TYPES OF RHYTHM

There are five types of rhythm associated with color: repetition, alternation, progression, continuation, and radiation. The purpose of rhythm is to provide an opportunity to move the viewer through the space, creating moments for emphasizing or downplaying various design elements. Color rhythm primarily evolves through color contrast of high and low saturation achieved through hue

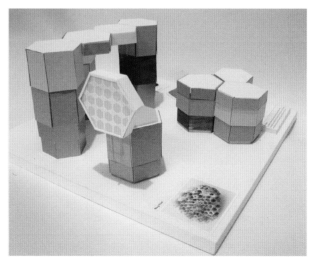

**FIGURE 4.5** "The Klatch." A versatile seating group inspired by a yellow-jacket wasp nest by student Julee Owens. Yellow textile pattern and material selections represent the colorations of the wasp and papery nest material.

## color + rhythm

**FIGURE 4.6** Bio-inspired color palettes.

(a) Color palette based on a graphic image of cactus in Ixtapa Zihuatanejo, State of Guerrero, Mexico. (© Pierre Arsenault/Alamy)

(b) Color palette based on a ring-necked parakeet.

(© imagebroker/Alamy)

(c) Color palette based on a passion flower vine. (© Miss Gracie B/Alamy)

(d) Color palette based on a Malachite butterfly.

(© Danita Delimont/Alamy)

(e) Color palette based on the bird of paradise flower. (© nagelestock. com/Alamy)

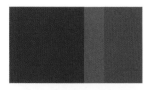

(f) Color palette based on foliage of the caladium plant.
(© Ros Drinkwater/Alamy)

(g) Color palette based on autumn season, Vermont.
(© Jon Arnold Images Ltd/Alamy)

# color + rhythm

sequence, value sequence, or multiple-color sequence. A strong contrast of color will create a dynamic, active, and spatially intense experience. If, on the other hand, we were to reduce the separation of chroma, the space would appear passive and static. These principles apply whether you're working in hue, value, or chroma contrasts. A row of columns or arches, a continuous line of crown molding, or the alternating pattern of colored mosaic tiles are examples of the many ways musical timbre is imitated in our built environment. The analyses of any interior space will uncover the use of at least one if not multiple types of rhythm. Each rhythm type can work independently or in combination with other types to create further visual interest to unify the visual composition.

In Figure 4.7a, the staircase incorporates two rhythmic concepts of progression and repetition highlighted in a vibrant red hue contrasting against the light gray wall and black tile floor. The design for the stair railing painted black uses line to accentuate vertical movement of the stair. The grid structure in front of the stair introduces a second repetitive concept with the negative square space and positive rectangular colonnade. The tension created between the foreground and stair is emphasized with the intense, powerful red, as if the stairs are being squeezed between the two these two forms. This example of rhythm illustrates great contrast of design further supported with color. If we switch the red stair coloring and foreground wall color, notice the emphasis is reversed and the rhythm is focused more on the lines created by the colonnade (Figure 4.7b). If we remove all color, the two rhythms are weakened (Figure 4.7c). In your design projects, try applying the chosen colors in different locations within various room mockups to see what happens to the overall design. This is a great test to see if you have placed color in the context that best suits both the color and the planned design.

As you read further and we discuss each color rhythm type, refer to Figure 4.8. These illustrations provide a simple visual dictionary of the various color rhythms discussed below. Keep in mind in any color selection processes for rhythm, lighting levels need to be considered as part of the desired effect. The brighter the lighting levels, the stronger the visual reaction will be to the color rhythm. Dimmer light will produce a more subtle result.

**63**

**FIGURE 4.7** (a) The staircase incorporates the rhythmic concepts of progression and repetition which are emphasized with a vibrant, red hue. (© Fancy/Veer/Corbis)

(b) Color rhythm emphasis is reversed and placed on the repetitive square design of the colonnade.

(c) No single particular rhythm is emphasized with hue or contrast.

## Repetition

**Repetition** is the systematic orderly succession of identical design elements (shape, line, color, form) along a define path in space. The Guggenheim Museum in New York City by Frank Lloyd Wright uses undulating, curvilinear forms for the sculptural ramp that leads the eye upward and around the interior space. The absence of color emphasizes the design, with natural light penetrating the volume and adding light and dark contrast (Figure 4.9).

Repeating similar elements will create visual unity within an interior space, whereas too much variation could create chaos and confusion. When using a particular color scheme (monochromatic: 1, complementary: 2, triadic/split complementary: 3, or tetrad: 4), the number of hues that form these color harmonies need to be repeated throughout the room to create rhythm and balance adequately. Attention should be paid to variations in value, intensity and warm versus cool hues. Too many hues assigned within the space will distort the visual rhythm and undermine the effectiveness of other design principles planned for the same space (balance and harmony). Rhythmic order is essential when color is applied to forms, shapes, and the organized structure of the interior environment. The work of an interior designer should support and strengthen the interior structure, not distract from or alter the intended design purpose. This can be minimized by placing color on key design elements or areas of larger proportion to downplay the rhythmic turmoil. Too much visual movement and users of the space may end up disoriented and confused (see Figure 4.10). The eye will need a place to rest. In every project we should seek "to build color rhythms into design as opportunities offer" (Ellinger, 1980, p. 97).

## color + rhythm

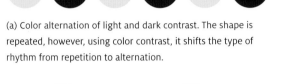

(a) Color alternation of light and dark contrast. The shape is repeated, however, using color contrast, it shifts the type of rhythm from repetition to alternation.

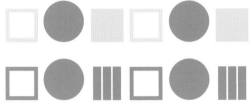

(b) Color continuity, in this example, is achieved by carrying the similar hue throughout the composition to connect dissimilar elements and create a more fluid rhythm.

(c) Progression using value from light to dark.

(d) Repetition by similarity in shape and hue.

(e) Color alternation through complementary hues, warm/cool contrast, and shape.

(f) Progression through size and value.

**FIGURE 4.8**

**FIGURE 4.9** Top. The Guggenheim Museum, in New York City, designed by Frank Lloyd Wright. (Courtesy of Condé Nast Publications, Inc.)

**FIGURE 4.10** Right. Example of "rhythmic turmoil." The Emperor Moth Boutique in Mayfair, London. (© Morley von Sternber/Arcaid/Corbis)

**FIGURE 4.11** Top. Interior of Wolfsburg Church, Germany, uses light and dark color contrast to break the space and add visual rhythm to the interior ceiling. (© Adam Woolfitt/Corbis)

**FIGURE 4.12** Left. Striped tile work in a contemporary bathroom accentuates movement both vertically and horizontally around the space. (© Scott Van Dyke/Beateworks/Corbis)

## Alternation

**Alternation** occurs when two design elements are repeated in sequence similar to repetition; however, the difference is that the pattern includes two distinctly different elements (round to square, red to blue) as opposed to one element repeating. Successive, alternating, horizontal bands of color can be used to compress the verticality of space.

In Figure 4.11, the Wolfsburg Parish Church (1960–1962) by architect Alvar Aalto located in Lower Saxony, Germany, is a good example of using alternating bands of color to break the vastness of the church nave. If you were to remove the white bands, the result would be a dark ominous ceiling that lacked the original movement toward the alter that Aalto intended. The dark contrast of the ceiling to the walls still provides a slight indication of the curving line, which can be removed altogether by removing the value shift from light to dark and reducing the color contrast with the interior walls. In Figure 4.12, the alternating horizontal bands of blue and brown create both vertical and horizontal movement. If the contrast between the two colors were minimized, the movement would be lessened. The two colors complement each other well, neither too intense nor overwhelming one another. However, if the contrast or saturation between two hues is intensified between the edge and transition of two colors, the resulting **vibrancy** or perception of movement could become overstimulating and thus compromise the type of rhythm applied to the design solution. The example in Figure 4.13 illustrates the concept of vibrancy that could result due to the high contrast of the two opposing complementary hues. In Figure 4.14a, the interior red carpeting is potentially too strong for this long corridor. The color is repeated on the ceiling above and contrasted with patterns from the green marble alone with the wood walls that overwhelm the space. In contrast, the corridor in Figure 4.14b uses less intense color combined with subtle pattern in the wood walls, creating a more inviting and pleasant space.

## Progression

**Progression** involves the repetition of similar elements with a continuous change (large to small, low to high, narrow to wide, light to dark). Progression

# color + rhythm

**FIGURE 4.13** Left. Using high-saturated opposing color creates strong vibrancy, resulting in an overly visually stimulating entrance to parking garage elevator.

(© weberfoto/Alamy)

**FIGURE 4.14** (a) Bottom left. Intense red flooring coupled with green marble and heavily patterned wood grain create an overly stimulating interior experience. (b) Bottom right. Subtle color intensity and material pattern result in a more pleasing interior experience.

(Bottom left and right: © Ferenc Szelepcsenyi/Alamy)

or sequencing of color rhythm can open up or close in space, depending on the contrast levels and number of hues used. For instance, when spaces are rather narrow or confined, using color rhythm enables to viewer's eye to move continuously through, giving the perception of widening space. In Figure 4.15, the bands of colored light behind the curved glass block progressing from warm to cool hues draws you in and around the space. By running the bands of color vertically instead of horizontally, your eye moves toward the ceiling of the space where additional design details are present.

Color rhythm in an interior should be created to gradually move the eye sequentially from one hue to the next or from one design element to the next.

Without color and pattern, the lack of rhythm that creates the perception of visual texture can also leave a space dull and uninspiring (Figure 4.16a). When color is introduced with strong geometry for pattern applied to the rug, wall surfaces, and ceiling, we can increase the rhythmic pattern and reinforce a clear design concept (Figure 4.16b).

Our goal is to create visual movement that connects all the parts of the whole. When the eye is forced to stop or unable to find a point of interest or repeating pattern, the result will be displeasing to the user of the space. When considering the use of different patterns or colored hues to create visual texture and movement, be cautious and avoid overwhelming the design.

**FIGURE 4.15** Opposite page. Progression of warm- and cool-colored fluorescent lights filter through the curving glass block wall at Dulles International Airport, Washington, D.C. (© Wiskerke/Alamy )

**FIGURE 4.16** (a) Left. With color and pattern missing, this hotel lobby waiting area is devoid of rhythm, creating a visually uninteresting space. (b) Right. The addition of color and pattern carries the eye around the lobby space, adding texture and visual interest to the space. (Illustrations by Steven Stankiewicz)

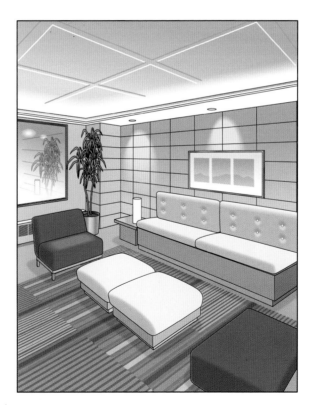

## Continuation or Transition

**Color continuation** refers to the placement of one or more colors throughout an interior to create a continuous movement of the eye through the space. It is the "fluid connection among composition parts" (Stewart, 2002, pp. 3–5). This concept is important for creating a sense of rhythm. Remember, our goal is to keep the viewer's eye moving. Referring back to Figure 4.8b, note that the top example is confusing because of compositional elements that are varied in shape and color. Using color continuity with each shape, the previously unrelated elements now share similarity and allow the eye to easily focus on each element and move continuously through the design. Whether this is done with a combination of curving, fluid lines or sharp, contrasting shapes, color is ultimately applied to visually animate forms and to bring liveliness to space and place. The rhythm sequence will send visual messages to indicate the mood or emotional movement of the interior, and it will evoke the spatial experience you wish the user to have. If we were to apply cool greens and blues to a series of curvilinear and circular shapes and forms moving through a space, this might be calming and restful. If this were a busy, active, working environment, the experience would contradict the desired outcomes—productivity and vigilance—workers may become lethargic and less productive. However, applied to a spa or health-care space, the use of color, shape, and rhythm would be appropriate for calming the guests. The key here is to make sure the selected colors, shapes, and sequence of shapes create rhythmic patterns related to one another for maximum effectiveness.

**FIGURE 4.17** Top. Radial pattern supported by complementary colors orange and blue. (© Bare Essence Photography/Alamy)

**FIGURE 4.18** Left. Assigning a yellow-orange hue to the interior columns complements the blue-violet interior and reinforces by contrast the radial pattern created by the interior design. (© Construction Photography/Corbis)

## Radiation

Color **radiation** uses a concentric color arrangement instead of objects to unify design elements and create visual movement versus the traditional sense where it is an arrangement of objects in a radial pattern. Figure 4.17 is an example of interior color radiation (notice the natural concentric pattern similar to a sunflower or pineapple). The orange dome over the Qur'an & Manuscripts Gallery at the Islamic Arts Museum Malaysia incorporates a palette of deep oranges and aqua blue to support the rhythmic pattern with complementary contrast.

In Figure 4.18, the orange columns arranged in a radial pattern accentuate this complementary contrast. If the column color was removed and replaced with the predominant blue-violet hue, the radial pattern would no longer be as evident and supported in the architectural plan in order to move the visitor around the perimeter of the space.

## Color and Line as Rhythm

Color can be used with line to "outline" a space; an effective and easy way to introduce rhythm to an interior that is limited in visual movement. This can be achieved with ceiling molding painted in a contrasting color to the walls, or with more detailed trellis work that provides a grid pattern and alternation of rectangular shapes. The contrast will focus viewers' attention on the use of line as a design element, moving their eyes around the space in which it is applied. Using a contrasting color both horizontally and vertically in the trellis and wall surface will highlight the design and the introduced movement. Adding complexity on a wall also reinforces its presence; in this case, affording users a sense of enhanced privacy, which aids their ability to relax. Compare the difference between Figures 4.19a and 4.19b; utilizing the element line with subtle contrasts in earthy green hues and dark wood achieves rhythm and the desired mood for this relaxing massage room.

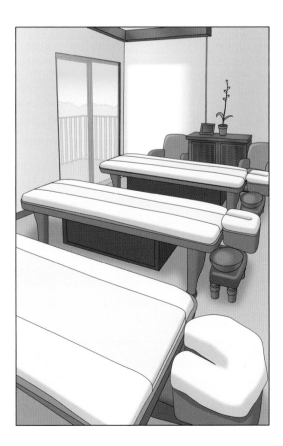

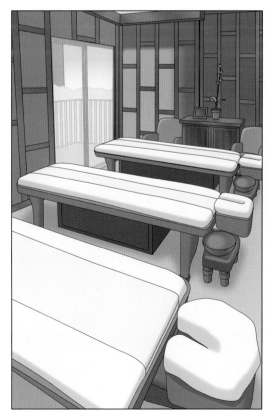

**FIGURE 4.19** (a) Left. Consideration of color and pattern is required if this massage room is to become a space for relaxation and meditation. (b) Right. Using natural greens and the line reminiscent of a wooded forest creates visual interest and movement for this massage room. (Illustrations by Steven Stankiewicz)

## FINAL THOUGHTS ON RHYTHM AND HUE

Color can also be applied to spaces to diminish design elements perceived as inhospitable. We've discussed that strong hues are associated with right angles and straight lines. Applying values of blue, green, and violet would therefore reduce and soften the rigid impression of the design. Awkward designs elements, unpleasing interior compositions, and permanent interior architectural features can be minimized by limiting value contrast and avoiding colors high in saturation. This technique is valuable when designers are renovating interior spaces and must contend with certain architectural features in existing buildings or structures that cannot be changed or removed.

**FIGURE 4.20**
Overuse of pattern and color distracts from the interior design of the space and its furnishings.
(© Elizabeth Whiting & Associates/Alamy)

Combine the various shapes presented in this chapter and repeat them in any one of multiple methods discussed to create an array of patterns that can be incorporated into your design. Textiles, wall coverings, and carpets are materials that present the opportunity to incorporate various patterns into a design scheme. A good rule of thumb when selecting patterns for an interior is to balance the scale with large and small patterns—a mixture of curvilinear or free-flowing designs, contrasted against more geometric designs (you may choose one type or both), that incorporates solids to give the eyes a place to rest. It is your decision which patterns receive the greatest attention based on scale. Just remember, too much pattern introduces too much rhythm and can easily overwhelm a space (Figure 4.20).

When working color into a rhythmic pattern, consider that interior design, like two-dimensional art, is subjective and speculative. There are rules when needed, but intuition and creativity must also be supported and valued. With the rules of color rhythm in mind, place hues at regular intervals for an orderly, calm, relaxing environment. Avoid sudden changes in the size and spacing of colored values unless the desired effect is an energetic and vibrant space. High-contrast colors combined with complex visual patterns and rhythms can diminish a room's apparent spatial volume. The outcome could be claustrophobic, cramped, and unwelcoming. However, a restaurant where people linger in a seated position under low lighting might benefit from high contrasts. In health-care environments, visual contrasts could add anxiety to already stressful situations that bring users to the space. In these cases, consider the length of time a person will be exposed, as this could have negative impact on one's mood and successful use of the space. Here are some tips to remember when using rhythm and hue:

- Highlight important architectural and interior elements (columns, coffered ceilings, furnishings, etc.).
- Use color as a tool to signal users regarding where to look first to orient their position in the space (wayfinding).
- Create positive or negative emotions using color psychology, as mentioned in Chapter 2.

# color + rhythm

- Organize the design elements into a compositional whole.
- Group design elements together, or isolate them completely.

## KEY WORDS

Rhythm, wayfinding, bio-inspired, repetition, alternation, vibrancy, progression, color continuity, radiation

## LEARNING OUTCOMES

- Rhythm and color can be used to create five types of visual effect: repetition, alternation, progression, continuation, and radiation.
- An interior space absent of visual movement can be supported with multiple color shifts in hue, value, and intensity to create a desired rhythmic order.
- Outlining with color is a way to add visual movement with minimal effort to impact the overall design.
- The stronger the contrast of color, the stronger the color rhythm.
- The weaker the contrast of color, the weaker the color rhythm.
- A color rhythm of more than three hues should be avoided due to visual clutter. The exception would be a gradual succession of light to dark values.
- Lighting levels should be considered in addition to the color to achieve the desired rhythmic pattern.
- Repeat a series of similarly shaped objects with contrasts between the repeating elements to create a regular color rhythm.
- Repeat a series of progressively larger elements with more dramatic contrasts between each design element for a progressive, dynamic color rhythm.

- Repeat a color hue with a repeating shape to create a calming, even pattern of movement.
- Repeat the same element in the same position on wall, floor, and ceiling surface in a space to unify the composition.

## EXERCISES

1. Using the drawing and shape tools in Microsoft Word, Adobe Illustrator, or colored papers, generate a series of rhythmic patterns using color and shape. Create one for each of the five types of rhythm discussed in the chapter: repetition, alternation, progression or sequencing, continuation or transition, and radiation.

2. Locate any designed object (building, furniture, appliance, electronic device, interior space, light fixture, etc.) whose influence was derived from the natural environment. Find a picture of this natural form, and analyze how the shape and color rhythm were used in the design. How does the color support the rhythmic order and impart meaning?

3. Select four to six pictures from design publications of interior spaces that use different types of rhythms mentioned in the chapter. Analyze what types are used, how they are used, and what effect they have on the space (volume, scale, proportion). In each example, analyze how color plays a role in amplifying or adding to the effect.

color + emphasis

5

All design principles are important; however, the significance of contrast is essential to users knowing their whereabouts in space. Emphasis is like the lighthouse that guides the boat safely to shore. For the designer, **emphasis** is a tool for creating points of interests not only for aesthetic purpose but to orient users of the space. I want to impress upon you that the principles of design are critical to functional design. Notice I did not use the overly used term "good design," because no design is either good or bad—only some designs function more efficiently than others. If any design principles, elements, and combinations thereof are used incorrectly, the overall design will suffer and ultimately not be appreciated by our clients.

*Enter color*—color attracts attention. It is the first thing that a person registers before object recognition is processed. Applying the strength of color to a particular area of a space or design element can bring greater attention to important features within our built environment. Color informs, and emphasis guides the user's attention to deliver an intended message. For example, a hotel plan would optimally draw your attention to its reception desk first. A dark mahogany base against a light beige backdrop is inviting and also conveys comfort and luxury.

Emphasis is an important design principle critical to all design disciplines, including interior design, architecture, landscape architecture, mixed media art, and fashion design. Emphasis is the direct method of establishing a point of visual interest. "Emphasis is the stressing of a particular area of focus rather than the presentation of a maze of details of equal importance. When a composition has no emphasis nothing stands out . . . the effective use of emphasis calls attention to important areas" (Bernard, 2008, ¶ 1).

Careful attention should be paid to where the visual emphasis is to be directed. Given physical movement through space, a focal point can be the intended destination. The path along that route is the journey, and once the destination has been reached, what do you intend for the user to experience? With seating, emphasis may be on a fireplace, a showcased piece of artwork (sculpture, painting), or a grouping of furniture. How does the destination affect the total

design? Are we redirected away from other critical visual information? How does the focal point support the overall design concept? These are a few important questions to ask when deciding what element in our interior to feature. The role of the designer when using the principle of emphasis is to analyze the interior space to determine what hierarchy of importance the content has. Once this is determined, concepts can be generated that carry out these intended functions and goals. It is too easy for an eager, young designer to select and apply visual importance to too many design features. Use a bit of restraint and avoid overemphasizing—no one element should demand 100 percent of the user's attention, or the remaining elements of your design are lost and serve no real purpose. "If you try to emphasize everything, you effectively emphasize nothing" (McNeil, 2007, ¶ 1). The interior designer should evaluate those individual architectural elements that have the highest priority based on programming information and assign the appropriate combination of the elements and principles of design to achieve the desired emphasis. **Programming** is one of the stages within the design process where you begin the data collection for a particular project. At any stage in the process, client feedback and input should be sought. Following are general questions you can begin to use when gathering information during the programming phase of a design project.

1. What type of space are you planning (waiting area, business office, living room, dining room)?
2. On average, how much time per day will you be spending in this space?
3. How many people will be using this space at any given time?
   You may need to consider age and gender ranges in this question.
4. What types of activities will be performed in this space (writing, reading, working at a computer, conversation, meetings, etc.)?
5. Does the space provide natural, artificial, or a combination of lighting types?
6. Are there preexisting aspects of the design that cannot be removed or altered?
   In this question, you may need to determine if the color can be changed even if the design feature cannot. For instance, if there is a wood floor, can

it be refinished? If it is a marble or terrazzo floor, this will be an important point of consideration in determining and working a new color scheme. Cost in the later phases is a key aspect that will determine the final outcome. It is much easier to apply a color or finish to materials than to remove and replace with new. Always know your boundaries and constraints on a project. In the design industry, it is rarely carte blanche. A great designer knows how to work within these constraints and achieve the client's goals.

7. What colors appeal and do not appeal to you? (Ask every member involved in the use of the space.)

If you are designing for one or two people, a question on color preferences for each individual is acceptable. If it is a space to be used by 10 to 20 people, you can take a color inventory of preferences and look for commonalities among the group that may lead to an appropriate color scheme that satisfies the group. If the space is used by 50 or more people, there are two workable scenarios: (1) Select a palette that is appropriate for the activity of the space, and use accent colors in places of socialization or areas of frequent interaction that do not receive extended periods of use. This might be an accent wall in a corridor, entrance, or conference room. (2) Prepare two or three color palettes and have the client select from your choices. Be careful not to prepare too many alternatives or your client may find it difficult to decide.

You will learn to build on these questions and modify them as needed depending on the project type you are working on. Each of these questions will influence color decisions. The questionnaire can be used whether you are designing for commercial or residential spaces.

Unlike artwork, which is primarily a static form of visual experience where the work is revealed to us all at once, interiors are experienced on multiple layers and levels. We move through our environments experiencing elements simultaneously. In multilevel spaces, our experience is different on each level, as well as places for repose where one might look over a cantilevered ledge to the people below; in this instance, the bird's eye view gives the user a sense of spaciousness, ascendency, freedom of choice, and spectatorship. Because of this multisensory experience of space, emphasis has the potential to change and morph. Unlike an object on a wall, we can move around above or below an element. The point to be made is that when using emphasis, consider it from the multiple perspectives the user might possibly be able to see. Each vantage point will create different opportunities of the interactive experience. "The aesthetic intent is to uplift the awareness of the viewer" (Zelanski & Fisher, 1995, p. 73).

## EMPHASIS WITH CONTRAST

One of the key principles of color use for design is contrast. Wong (1997, p. 14) defines contrast as the "visual (characteristics of shape and color), dimensional, or quantitative differences that distinguish one shape, part of a shape, or group of shapes from another shape, another part of the same shape, or another group of shapes." The composition in Figure 5.1a illustrates no real visual distinctions other than different shapes. In this example, no unique shape or color is emphasized. If we alter one shape by adding a color (Figure 5.1b), the hierarchy is established and the rectangle now has visual dominance within the composition.

Contrast can be used to draw attention to the most important elements in the interior environment and can add variety to the overall design. Depending on clients' needs, the scale of the project, or the design type, the interior designer may choose to draw attention to certain elements through the deliberate control of contrast. When used, it features a particular design element as the dominant or focal point. There are a variety of methods for creating visual emphasis through contrast, including isolation, placement, and dominance or focal point.

Artist Shirl Brainard (2003, p. 119) identifies several types of contrast that are applicable to the interior environment:

- Contrast of position or location in relation to other design features (asymmetrically placed).
- Contrast of size to other design features (large/small).

- Contrast of value (light/dark).
- Contrast of color (*hue:* red vs. green; *saturation:* bright vs. dull).
- Contrast of shape and form (a circular form amidst a grouping of rectilinear forms).
- Contrast of textures (soft to hard, smooth to rough, texture to texture).
- Contrast of anomaly, defined as a "deviation from the norm" (Brainard, 2003, p. 119). An example of this technique could be an antique chair positioned within a modern space, where styles contrast, but the single chair draws attention as different from the "norm."

Emphasis can be generated with any one of these techniques, and several can be combined to create a more visually interesting point of dominance in your projects. If everything is of equal emphasis, there is no contrast. Early studies conducted on color and aesthetics indicate that "individual choices differed most with respect to hue and that pairs showing strong contrasts were preferred" (Ball, 1965, p. 442).

## Color Emphasis through Location and Isolation

By alienating a particular design element from its surroundings, we can increase its visibility and importance. In Figure 5.2, the orange cantilevered "coloured play pod of the waiting area" at the Richard Desmond Children's Eye Centre in London designed by Penoyre & Prasad "bursts through the floor above" and floats amiss a wave of external louvers (Commission for Architecture and the Built Environment, 2008, ¶ 3). In terms of visual emphasis based on the individual spectral hues, orange has been graded as the color with most visibility, followed by yellow, green, red, and blue (Ball, 1965, p. 445). Depending on the spatial characteristics (large or small volume, abundant or limited light, other hues and materials and their level of lightness or darkness, and proportions), the relative brightness of the individual hues in full saturation will vary in degree of emphasis. This applies more when making color decisions for existing interior conditions and you do not have the flexibility to make changes to the space. On the

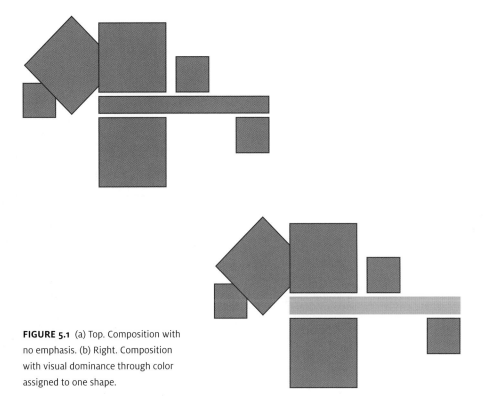

**FIGURE 5.1** (a) Top. Composition with no emphasis. (b) Right. Composition with visual dominance through color assigned to one shape.

**FIGURE 5.2** Left. The Richard Desmond Children's Eye Centre at Moorfields Eye Hospital in London. High drama created with a bright, orange hue features this remarkably unusual architectural form against the building's façade. (© G Jackson/Arcaid/Corbis)

**FIGURE 5.3** Top. Hotel lounge in the Burj Al Arab Hotel. Rich colors, reflective material, and strong contrasts emphasize the luxuriousness of the space. (© Massimo Listri/Corbis)

**FIGURE 5.4** Royal Academy of Arts Restaurant, Burlington House, London. Nighttime interior with (a) top, bar in foreground and red light setting; (b) middle, blue light setting; and (c) bottom, magenta light setting. Each create a distinct nuance as part of the dinning experience. (Top, middle, and bottom: © Arcaid/Alamy)

other hand, consider the apparent shifts in color intensity relative to the features and elements you are designing and the color planned for this particular design feature. In Figure 5.3, the light washing the banquet seating of this hotel lounge diffuses the intensity of the yellow-gold upholstery. The gold scroll pattern in the flooring is intensified in brightness when surrounded by a darker-colored field of color. The metallic finishes used throughout the space take on different intensities as the lighting reflects from their surfaces. In this space, scale and contrast of value in the carpet pattern and ceiling detail generate the main focal point.

Isolating color is an additional way for applying the concept of emphasis. Rather than using a colored material or media to accentuate a particular design feature, you can use colored light from incandescent bulbs, fluorescent tubes, halogens, and floodlights, to name a few, or from the use of colored gels applied to the rim of a light fixtures to filter a specific color. Using light to lightly wash or graze a wall surface can add a dominant feature at low cost and allow the space to change at the owner's will. In Figure 5.4a, the nighttime interior of the restaurant and bar at the Royal Academy of Arts Restaurant, in London, uses colored light to emphasize the decorative, coffered ceiling. The light is set against an interior layout with low contrasting materials in an **achromatic** palette to provide a simple background as the subdominant feature, so the colored light remains the focal point. Additional emphasis is added to the ceiling with a lighting system that slowly changes color to create different experiences (Figures 5.4b and 5.4c). The changing spectrum of light also alters the visual perception of the space, with each color rendition creating a unique experience. Figure 5.5a is another example where progression of different-colored lights adds direction with (rhythm) drawing the visitor inward.

FIGURE 5.5 (a) Left. Colored light used to draw viewers into as well as accent the space, which is limited in color or texture contrast. (b) Bottom. In this example, we've removed the colored light to illustrate how the illumination created a much-needed ambiance, visual interest, and sense of direction in the space. (Left: © Iconotec/Alamy)

The darker blue compared to the other hues pulls the viewer's attention toward the back of this space. The advancing red hue and light value of green contrast with the darker blue value. If this space lacked a color assignment, the emphasis and visual importance would be removed (Figure 5.5b).

## Contrast of Hue and Value

For contrast of hue, select colors that are opposite one another on the color wheel. Using color at full intensity is a very striking method for forming interesting focal points. The colors of lower intensities are more subtle and are enjoyed for secondary elements or general room use. As colors become less intense and lighter, the contrast factor diminishes and contrast for dominance is more difficult to attain. Refer back to Figure 2.10a in Chapter 2 to refresh lessons on contrast levels.

**FIGURE 5.6a** Color is a key element for branding and marketing a business image. This space lacks color for potential clients to make a visual association and connection with the firm.
(Illustration by Steven Stankiewicz)

**FIGURE 5.6b** The simple and dramatic use of red-orange draws a clear focal point to the key design element within the space, while the gray provides necessary balance of the bright hue.
(Illustration by Steven Stankiewicz)

In Figure 5.6a, the conference space is dark, drab, and lacks necessary energy and stimulation required for brainstorming, conferencing, and corporate conversations to take place. Additionally, the space lacks "image" or an identifiable feature that a client might relate to the firm. The floor space is broken by the border; the horizontal bars require extension to the room's corners, as well as a higher level of contrast for stimulation. The introduction of a vibrant red-orange draws attention and emphasis to the video conferencing wall, while the surrounding gray slightly neutralizes the hue's effect to provide the eye with areas of rest. The conference table and credenza have been replaced with a cool gray to blend with interior surfaces (Figure 5.6b).

In Figure 5.7, the interior colonnades in a series of highly saturated spectrum colors contrast with each other as well with as the opposite window wall. The blue ceiling provides the needed unity; otherwise, the colored columns would be overwhelming and lack connection to the interior space. In this example, the scale allows for the saturated colors. A space on a smaller scale would be consumed by this application of intense color.

Value contrast is probably the easiest of the contrast types. A light/dark contrast of black, gray, or white values can emphasize without the use of chromatic (colored) hues. The residential staircase in Figure 5.8a is an example of value contrasts. The warm, dark, wood finish of the stair threads contrasts against the white

**FIGURE 5.7** Temasek Polytechnic, Singapore, 1991–1995. Architect: James Stirling, Michael Wilford and Associates. (© Arcaid/Alamy)

**FIGURE 5.8** (a) Top. Residential corridor using material for color and design contrast to emphasize the stairway. (b) Bottom. Removal of the color contrast eliminates the stair as a focal point. (Top: © Floresco Productions/Corbis)

**FIGURE 5.9** Left. Hampton Court, design by Claire Whitehouse. A circular brick arch gateway forms the focal point that leads into this residential space. (© John Glover/Alamy)

**FIGURE 5.10** Opposite page. Serpentine Pavilion, 2006, London. An inflatable balloon-like cloud canopy illuminates like the sky above the foam block café seating of the pavilion. The ivy panels surrounding the café were a collaborative project between German Artist Thomas Demand and Dutch Architect Rem Koolhaas. Demand modeled ivy constructed from colored paper and cardboard was later photographed and installed as wallpaper art. (© VIEW Pictures Ltd/Alamy)

walls, cabinetry, and furniture, adding to the visual importance of the design feature. If we were to remove the contrast, the stair no longer has any value or importance added (Figure 5.8b).

## Contrast of Design Feature (Shape and Form)

Graphically, emphasis can be established as hierarchy of information when the information is presented in alternative styles. When *reading* a line of <u>text</u>, there are several ways **emphasis** can be given to a word for added importance, including color. This added e m p h a s i s informs the reader that one phrase should be attended to more than another. Too much emphasis and individual elements fight for dominance. In this example, we contrasted various text styles with roman type. In Figure 5.9, the circular archway defines and frames the courtyard entrance, leading to the residence in the background, through contrasts of both design feature (form) and color. Also notice the mastery of symmetry in the front elevation.

## Contrast of Texture

Using color and texture contrasts (smooth vs. rough) can add emphasis. The London, England, Serpentine Pavilion 2006 by Dutch architect Rem Koolhaas in Figure 5.10 is a perfect example of mixing color and texture to create a dramatic effect. The textured blue contrasts nicely against an achromatic interior with smooth, slick surfaces.

FIGURE 5.11 (a) Top. International airport concourse requires color assigned to highlight specific interior details. (b) Bottom. Application of a split-complementary color scheme highlighting important interior surfaces. (Illustrations by Steven Stankiewicz)

## Emphasis with Color Dominance (Focal Point)

A **focal point** is a *single* design element that receives the greatest visual emphasis in a room. We use focal points to give the eyes a place for rest or contemplation. In terms of wayfinding, visitors to a space will usually be attracted to walk toward the focal point, which may be an art object, piece of furniture, or functional module such as a reception center. Unlike emphasis, which can have one or multiple elements contrasting, focal points stand alone from the crowd. Just as symmetrical balance draws your eyes to the center of a composition or room layout, so does color used with emphasis draw your attention to the color first and the object second.

Focal points can be achieved by isolation (placement), by highlight with contrast of shape, size, or color (which differentiates the element from its surroundings), or by implementing directional movement that leads the eye toward the element to be emphasized. This is accomplished using rhythmic properties discussed in Chapter 4 (progression, repetition) or other combinations of the above to create a focal point.

Compare the difference between the two color approaches to the interior of an international airport. The original illustration (Figure 5.11a) is an example of deconstructed geometry and sculptural design. The large mass of windows, broken by structural I-beams, frames the view from the interior concourse. Here the view as focal point and an interior in neutral grays yearns for color to highlight specific forms. In Figure 5.11b, a split complementary color plan placed in the foreground, middle ground, and background provide directional movement and focus through the concourse to the space beyond. The violet contrasted with the yellow-orange provides additional emphasis and draws attention to the space beyond. A slight increase in value assigned to the I-beams increases their distinction in the space, and the new hues result in a more comfortable scale and highlighting of specific interior forms.

Dominant color in a color scheme can accent the appearance of an item that previously received little visual attention, create visual enhancement in an architectural feature, or add a contrast of visual weight to something of importance (memorabilia, collectibles).

Rengel (2007), when he discusses emphasis, draws a dichotomy between dominance and distinctiveness. Dominance, as he defines it, can be realized by "size, intensity, or interest" (p. 187). Distinctiveness occurs when a focal object or area is noticeably different from its surroundings. In Figure 5.12, the spiral staircase and textured stone wall in the background are equally balanced. Each form is distinctive from its surrounding—the stair with its free-flowing form and the feature wall with a heavy texture; both design features use neutral hues visually highlighted by light and dark contrast.

## Contrast of Anomaly

An **anomaly** is an irregular deviation or departure from what one considers to be normal. In interior design, this takes the form of contrasting distinct styles where one becomes the focal point. Figure 5.13 shows a traditional residential interior with crown moldings, decorative objects, wood flooring, and traditional-styled chairs contrasted with the iconic Artichoke ceiling lamp designed by Poul Henningsen in 1958. The modern light fixture contrasts with the traditionally styled interior, even though it is set against a similar white background—it refuses to blend, and thus becomes a focal for this dining space.

## Color Contrast for Safety and Welfare

Contrast is preferred by viewers. Viewers need variety and interest among colors in their immediate surroundings. A complete lack of contrast can lead to lack of stimulation or direction, boredom, and difficulty processing visual cues in spaces where activity and alertness are important. This might include workplaces, class-

**FIGURE 5.12** Apray Courtyard, London. Architecture firm: Foster Partners.

(© VIEW Pictures Ltd/Alamy)

**FIGURE 5.13** This traditional interior contrasts through anomaly with a vintage mid-century modern artichoke pendant. (Getty Images/iStock Exclusive)

rooms, operating rooms, and areas where detailed work on machinery is being performed. Most interior designs require a certain amount of contrast to assist with differentiation between spatial planes and elements. Too much similarity of the components in any design becomes disorienting and limits the functionality of the space.

Especially in larger complex commercial spaces, visual signals are necessary for orientation and recognition of one's location within the interior. "Visual aids that use colors help us quickly and easily orient ourselves in buildings and spaces" (Meerwein, Rodeck, & Mahnke, 2007, p. 71). Color can become a visual map that allows you to recall specific places you have been based on color. Imagine your average American parking garage leading to your average American mega mall. Often patrons are encouraged to memorize their color-coded location, making it easier to return to. This type of design tool can be beneficial to the public at large, as well as to clients with special needs. In the case of patients with Alzheimer's disease, color recognition is a way to offset memory loss and provide a method of recall. A color-coded chest of drawers could help a patient know where to find articles of clothing in a series of drawers that might otherwise be difficult to distinguish in a standard wood-stained cabinet. The furniture piece takes on two functions—a colorful design feature and a functional tool for patients with memory loss.

Color can be used to emphasize the space type. "The coloration indicates not only its function but its identity; what one is likely to encounter; and in association, assumptions are made reading the type of people who are and will be visiting this place" (Smith, 2008, p. 317).

The covered entrance to the St. Louis Children's Hospital in Missouri uses brightly saturated hues. The colors and shapes indicate this is a place of care for children (Figure 5.14). The playfulness of the colors arranged in the familiar shape of a butterfly might relax incoming patients and add cheer. This covered space is also a good example of a color used to clearly demarcate an important access and egress point.

**FIGURE 5.14** Colorful entrance to the St. Louis Children's Hospital. (© David R. Frazier Photolibrary, Inc./Alamy)

## DESIGN TIPS

Trying to select what design feature or object to emphasize or make into a focal point in a project can pose a challenge. This is a good conversation to have with your client; the choice of emphasis can be based on a personal object or item the client has a historical connection with. In this case, the interior space should be worked around this object. If you are working on a project from the ground up, the cost of certain elements might dictate what items receive attention. An original Piet Mondrian wouldn't be placed in a location where you're sitting or standing facing away from the painting. In residential design, one of the common issues facing many home owners is the fight between the flat-screen television and the fireplace. Luckily, advances in entertainment technology have resolved this design dilemma—now, several hidden, recessed, or projected options for television mean a client won't have to compromise space for enjoyment of art objects or furniture. Here are some tips to guide you:

- Use the accent color sparingly; otherwise, it is no longer an accent and might be confused with the dominant color. Cluttered or overly saturated color detracts from meaning.

- Establish a recognizable amount of value or hue contrast for the design feature to generate attention.

- Keep in mind that a contrast of value will receive greater attention than contrast of different hues or saturation. Use the type of contrast that works for your individual project needs; this will vary from project to project. Emphasis can be subtle or extreme.

- Use a warm hue versus cool to increase the dominant effect. Remember, warm hues generally advance; therefore, receding cool colors would have a lesser impact visually.

- Use light to accentuate your dominant feature. Lighting coupled with color can enhance the drama of the focal point with reflection and shadow.

- In some instances, you may wish to downplay a particular design element. There will be situations where preexisting interior walls, structures, ceiling elements, or mechanicals are not removable and the visual attention they demand becomes a distraction. In this case, the use of **color-masking** techniques can lend unity to disorganization. Color masking involves hiding the design element with color using shading, color patterns, or blending with surroundings. A common application involves painting return air vents in the ceiling or walls the same color as their adjacent surroundings to hide them. As you study color, observe the many places where designers have used camouflage techniques to mask necessary objects that are not meant to be focal points. Keep in mind that residential clients will have different concerns about cosmetics than commercial clients, and solutions should be tailored to the environment and programmed use of the space.

When working on emphasis in your design work, the goal is to catch and hold the viewers' attention. Emphasis can be used to accent and isolate an object and, in turn, increase the perceived importance of that design element in the space. Color should be planned from the outset of the design process—and not be an afterthought. When color is considered for emphasis during planning, it is important to have mastered the various contrast methods that may "heighten the visibility and shift the meaning" of the space (Stewart, 2002, pp. 2–17). A designer must carefully consider all potential symbolism and meaning that users might interpret as they interact with the spaces they inhabit.

## KEY WORDS

Programming, contrast, emphasis, focal point, anomaly, color masking

## LEARNING OUTCOMES

1. Understand how color and contrast can create focal points in a space.

2. Texture, pattern, value, and color can all be used to create emphasis.

3. Emphasis is an important tool for wayfinding, assisting those with memory loss, and adding visual stimuli.

4. Color as emphasis can attract and hold the attention of its viewer.

5. Contrast of warm and cool colors when added to three-dimensional forms advance certain features, adding to the perceived importance of the object being highlighted.

6. Color selected and applied to a design feature and further isolated in the space by contrast can have more visual power than the actual object that is being colored.

7. Most people see color first, then the object.

8. Contrast should be given attention in the beginning of a color design project so that it can develop naturally.

## EXERCISES

1.  Locate several magazine photos of interior spaces or architectural exteriors. Describe how dominance and color contrast are used to highlight points of interest in an interior space. Select from several different design types to compare and contrast the strategies that have been used and how they relate to their intended functions.

2.  Locate three examples of focal points using color as the main driver for emphasis. Select from across several design disciplines (art, communication design, interior design, architecture).

3.  Generate a three-dimensional model of an interior (four walls, a ceiling, and a floor) using foam board, chip board, cardboard, or other forms of sturdy artist board, approximately 12 by 10 by 14 inches. Next, create a series of forms (spheres, cubes, cones, organic shapes) out of card stock, museum board, and so on. Using the methods described in this chapter, generate a few spatial studies examining how color emphasis can be applied and manipulated in your model. Use colored media (Color-aid, artist papers, or other colored material to generate your experiments). Try at least two or three variations. Compare and contrast what works well and what does not work well. Photograph your models.

4.  At your school, work, local shopping venue, or community hospital, document ways in which color is used as a communication device to visually inform, direct, and provide orientation and spatial recognition within your surroundings. Pay attention to color patterning on walls, floors, and ceilings, signage, color in art as a communication tool, design features that are emphasized, or color blocking (color-keyed to areas for recognition, i.e., the *blue room*). How might you use these same strategies in your own work?

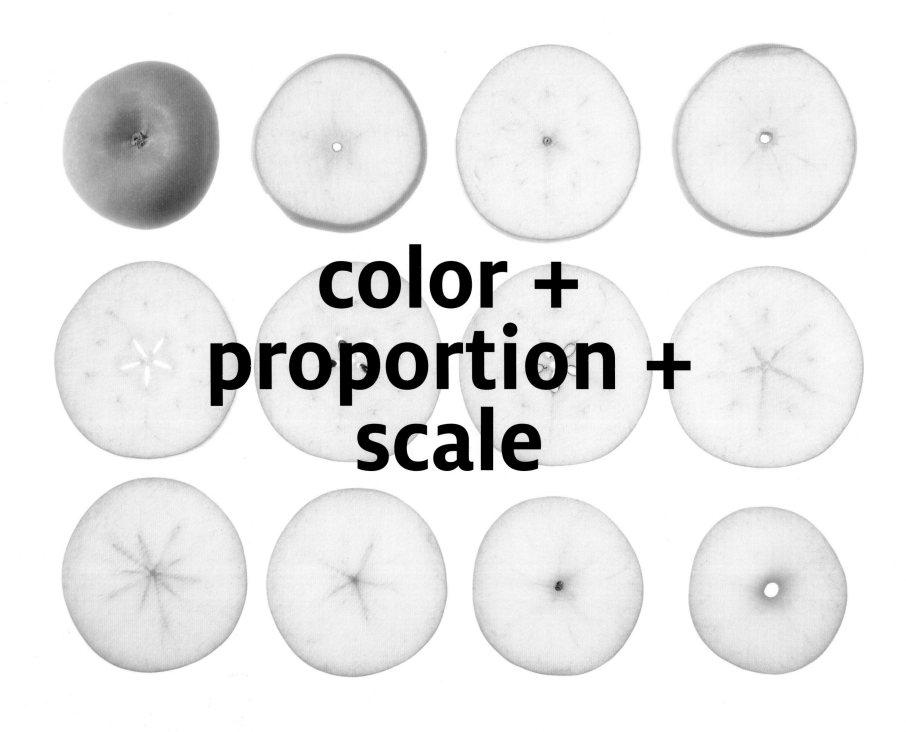

color +
proportion +
scale

6

**FIGURE 6.1** Top. The use of a human figure in this image establishes an estimated height of this chair at over 25 feet tall.
(© Clark Dunbar/Corbis)

**FIGURE 6.2** Right. Woman writing her "big ideas" with a big pencil.
(© Burke/Triolo Productions/ Brand X/Corbis)

Any subjective review of design considers proportion as one of the key elements that we use to rationalize and seek order in the things around us. The beauty we see in the natural world grows from the divine proportions that help to make sense of everything, a correctness or fitting of parts into a composition pleasing to the eye. **Proportion** is defined as the size relationships between elements (parts) and the visual composition or space (whole). Proportion and scale are much the same, are often confused with one another, and inevitably are used interchangeably. Although, they are not exactly synonymous, we cannot discuss one without the other. Proportion and scale are related in that you are using a hierarchy of color information where proportions will be given to the accent, followed by subdominant, and finally dominant color, or the color that appears within two-thirds of the space volume. Many times the two terms—proportion and scale—are combined when a designer is describing the relationships between one part of a design and another. **Scale** refers to the size of a shape in relation to a given known, in most cases, the human body and its position within space. Because we use our bodies to make comparison between various elements and physical activities, our world has been proportioned to accommodate the size and shape of our bodies. Figure 6.1 illustrates the need for human-to-object relationships in your design planning to establish the relative scale of the surroundings. If the human figure was removed, the scale of the chair would be in question, making it difficult to gauge further planning of additional design elements accurately. If our proportions were removed from the equation of design, the idea of function and aesthetics would be altered considerably. In Figure 6.2, the exaggerated proportion of a pencil relative to the human hand would limit the usability of this object; we can make an assessment that the proportions simply to do not "feel right" or "look right." However, for a sense of humor or youth, this is applicable in some scenarios. This natural intuition can be beneficial in working proportional color plans.

## COLOR AND PROPORTION

Color palettes can contain from one to five colors. Limiting the number of colors in an interior space is crucial for achieving balance and a unified composition.

Too much color can be overwhelming and compromise the intended communication of the design and its function; conversely, limiting color can elicit negative reactions of boredom, monotony, or general lack of interest in the design. Paint manufactures use proportions of paint when mixing color to get the desired hue. If the proportion is off, the color will be incorrect. This same principle applies to interiors; if the proportions are off, the desired effect will be compromised.

Through multiple modes of inquiry and experimentation, students will form a deeper understanding and connection to design theory at an earlier stage in their education. The grids provided in Figure 6.3 can be copied and used to generate your color proportions. Base color or dominant color makes up the ground or background of your space. The second and third colors are secondary or subdominant, and the smaller proportions are your accent colors. Another method for establishing proportion is the "rule of thirds."

Assign dominant and subdominant colors with accents for visual contrasts in your color plan. Keep these proportions in mind for a three-color scheme: 60 to 70 percent dominant, 20 to 30 percent subdominant, and 10 to 20 percent accent. Depending on the number of colors in your plan, these percentages may shift slightly. The various proportions of a given color will determine the physical sensation or perception. In Figure 6.4a, the color scheme uses a grid to proportion the five-hue palette. If we relocate the various hues assigned different proportion in the grid, the visual impact of the scheme changes (see Figure 6.4b). This tool can be valuable to gauge the overall sensation you are attempting to achieve within your interior space. An intensely bright color will dominate an interior; therefore, it is advantageous to use these hues for smaller areas of your interior and assign less saturated, lighter hues for larger areas of the space. Intense color will naturally draw attention and should be limited or balanced with its complement; avoid having a color overwhelm your design. From previous discussions, we know that the larger the color area, the lighter a color appears, and the smaller the color area, the darker it will appear. When preparing your proportions, these phenomena and the concepts mentioned in Chapter 3 (value, hue, intensity, etc.) should be taken into consideration. Many variables are combined when we work

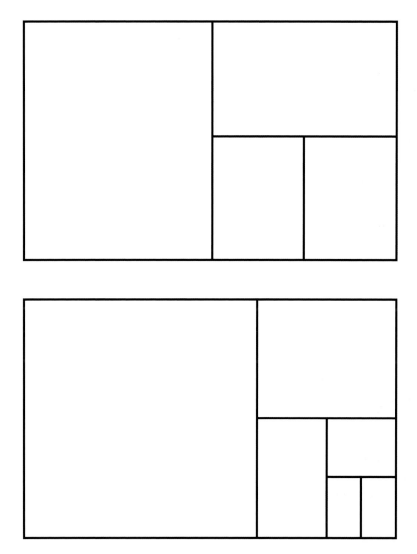

**FIGURE 6.3** Grid proportion using the Fibonacci Sequence. These can be used for initial color planning and comparison of proportions. As you progress in your color studies this will become natural and automatic.

**FIGURE 6.4** (a) Left. Five-color plan arranged to evaluate proportioned color strength and relationship. (b) Right. Color plan illustrating perceptual changes in color language when proportions are reassigned.

**FIGURE 6.5** Vivid color and strong geometry blend to reduce this space's large volume.

(© Art on File/Corbis)

with color; this is precisely why every step should be taken to address all possibilities of color change and manipulation early in the color-planning process.

Architect Janet Ford suggests that as we prepare our color proportions, we should keep in mind that "our eyes perceive a visual mix . . . and the mix will differ depending on the proportions of allocated areas" (2007, ¶ 1). She goes on to identify six key elements to consider for color proportioning:

- The color with the largest proportional area is the dominant color (the ground).
- Smaller areas are subdominant colors.
- Accent colors are those with a small relative area but offer a contrast because of a variation in hue, intensity, or saturation.
- To create an accent, place small areas of light color on a dark background, or a small area of dark on a light background.
- If large areas of a light hue are used, the whole area will appear light; conversely, if large areas of dark values are used, the whole area appears dark.
- Alternating color by intensity rather than proportion will also change the perceived visual mix of color.

The proportion of color will be relative to other design elements and should be scaled to fit interior spaces on a situation-by-situation basis. Red can be overwhelming as a dominant color in a small space; a larger space with adequate natural light can handle a strong color in large quantities. Color, contrast, and spatial volume must work together to create the intended effects for the spaces purpose and its users.

The University of California, San Francisco Mission Bay Community Center, designed by architects Legorreta + Legorreta in 2005, is colored in a saturated blue and accentuated with geometric shapes, forming a sculpturally inviting space (see Figure 6.5). The volume is accentuated by a single hue, with natural light filling the space from above and making the dark, strong, cobalt blue less overwhelming. The hue is contrasted against the puce (brownish-purple) flooring, creating the needed harmony. The sheer volume of the space is slightly reduced using geometric patterns along the wall to break the massive field of blue.

The modern living space in Figure 6.6a is predominantly neutral, with a few touches of color contrasts from the armchairs and artwork located above the sofa. In this example, the geometry of the space highlights the interior design, but our attention is not focused because of the limited color contrast with other design elements in the room. The adage "a small amount of color can go a long way" in an interior space may hold true for most; however, too little, and the color that is used may seem arbitrary and insignificant. If color is not planned, whether the color of the materials or the applied color (paints, wall coverings, textiles, etc.), the resulting space may lack character and visual significance.

There is a need to assign color to add distinction but also to create a more intimate proportion for the living space. In Figure 6.6b, localized color has been placed to change our spatial perception of the interior proportions. The vertical column separating the living and dining space has increased in value and in the repetitive square forms on the wall leading into the dining room. The added

**FIGURE 6.6** (a) Top. Living space with limited color, contrast, and variety. (b) Bottom. Recoloration of the living space introduces strong hues for added drama and decreased proportion and scale.

(Illustrations by Steven Stankiewicz)

contrast pulls the living space inward, creating a more intimate conversation space as well as adding a dramatic, darker red that contrasts with the sofa and artwork. Notice how this has changed the visual perceived proportion, brightness, and articulation of design elements of the space compared to the original illustration.

In certain situations, an exaggerated proportion may be needed; in this case, proportion and emphasis are united as a means to drawing attention to a particular design element. As shown in Figure 6.7, Spanish architect Santiago Calatrava used mass scale in the Quadracci Pavilion at the Milwaukee Art Museum. The volume is exaggerated, giving the visitors the sensation of endlessness as the interior frames and reflects the lake waters beyond. The May West lips sofa created in 1972 by Salvador Dali and Jean-Michel Frank is an excellent example of whimsical humor that can be extended through exaggeration of proportion. In Figure 6.8, the Mae West Lips Sofa designed by Salvador Dali in 1937 is shown in the reception area of the Sanderson Hotel in London designed by Philippe Starck.

**FIGURE 6.7** Top. Scale and volume are increased in the interior of the Quadracci Pavilion by Santiago Calatrava, Milwaukee Art Museum, with the use of natural light, low contrast, and light-colored materials. (© Chuck Eckert/Alamy)

**FIGURE 6.8** Right. The Sanderson Hotel, London. "Lips" sofa in reception area. Architect: Philippe Starck. (© Arcaid/Alamy)

Although we are examining the principles of design separately to better understand how to use color in design, all these elements ultimately work together, simultaneously achieving the final result. Only by examining them independently can you see the intricacy of how they work and then be able to execute more successful color design solutions.

## COLOR AND SCALE

Whereas proportion is concerned with the relationships of various parts arranged to create an aesthetically pleasing whole, scale is concerned with the relative size of space (large, small, short, tall, narrow, wide). Color can be used to change our visual perception of a space's actual size.

Children live in an adult's world, where large spaces can seem overwhelming and frightening (Figure 6.9a). Color is critical in the classroom to reduce boredom and provide an environment that "improves visual processing, reduces stress, and challenges brain development through visual stimulation/relationships and pattern seeking" (Daggett, Cobble, and Gertel, 2008, p. 1).

In Figure 6.9b, the introduction of a color scheme that is energetic and stimulating has the potential to increase students' creativity, imagination, and ability and willingness to learn. The deep-blue horizontal line around the room's perimeter (1) divides the vertical height to a relatable scale for children and (2) relates and frames the two wooden storage units into the total design. The color also provides the needed dark contrast with the other hues. The darker blue on the bottom third of the space lowers the apparent ceiling height as an additional measure to make the space more comfortable for children.

The location of green to the ceiling and yellow to the upper observation balcony reduces the ceiling height and adds visual interest throughout the spatial

**FIGURE 6.9** (a) Top. This learning environment for young children lacks logical relationships, with its massive volume and scale. (b) Bottom. Careful color location decreases and breaks up the spatial volume, while introducing contrast and visual interest, and keeping young learners stimulated. (Illustrations by Steven Stankiewicz)

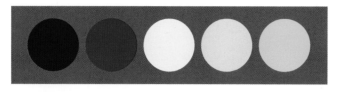

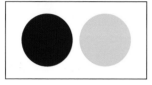

**FIGURE 6.10** Lighter hues appear to advance forward and have the ability to change perceived spatial scale.

volume. The addition of dark gray to the floor divides the space into zones so activity areas can be arranged and identified for the children. The primary initiative in the primary color plan is adding more variety and contrast to the space, therefore reducing the apparent visual scale. Additional texture or patterning was avoided in response to the workspaces and shelving ultimately being filled with books, toys, and games, providing the needed variety.

## Practical Applications with Color and Perception of Scale

Following are a few tips to keep in mind when working with color and scale:

- Light colors advance, and dark colors recede. Figure 6.10 illustrates this concept. The purple appears to recede into the gray field, whereas the yellow advances toward you. Does the yellow appear to be larger than the purple? In fact, they are the same.
- Use a hue in two to three close values. This will result in high contrast and separation of visual elements resulting in the perception of large space. Recall that Munsell's value scale "trunk" starts at the ground with black and moves upward to white. This principle relates to gravity, where color takes on the property of having perceived weight. When working in space, use this natural

order of value—darker values should be placed toward the bottom of the interior (the floor or approximately the bottom one-quarter or one-third of the space), middle values at the center, and the lightest values at the top. This will create a better sense of balance.

- A room with a dark ceiling and light floor will appear top-heavy and out of balance. Dark values when placed approximately 36 to 42 inches high on a wall will visually slice a room in half. If the ceiling is 8 or 9 feet high, this can be oppressive, whereas, applied to a high ceiling of 10 feet or more, the dark color can make an expansive space appear more intimate.
- Small spaces can be made to appear much larger if similar colors are used throughout, especially if they are keyed to the same floor covering color.
- Dark, strong, or warm colors like red or dark orange will make the wall seem to advance and make the room feel much smaller.
- Cool, dull, or light colors (reduction in chroma or value) will appear to stretch space—to push the wall outward. This can be achieved if the wall, floor, and ceiling colors are keyed to the same color.
- A long corridor will seem shorter if the end wall is painted or covered in a warm color, just as a small space will seem larger if all surfaces are painted the same white or neutral color. Washing the walls with light adds to this perception.
- A low ceiling will seem higher if it is painted a lighter value than the walls and emphasized with the use of crown molding around the perimeter of the room painted the same value as the walls. The crown will visually extend the wall, making the room appear taller.
- Large pieces of furniture will look smaller if upholstered in the same color value as the walls. The blending of visual edges diminishes the apparent weight. The same concept applies to darker upholstery against darker-valued walls. To increase the visual weight of a rather small piece of furniture, use opposing value and color contrasts.
- While the concept that warm colors advance and cool colors recede to make a space appear small or large is still fresh in our mind, let's not confuse the use

of dark hues with light hues. A dark hue, whether warm or cool, can decrease the apparent size of space, and, conversely, if the hue is light, whether warm or cool, it tends to visually open a space.

## ADDITIONAL METHODS FOR ESTABLISHING PROPORTIONAL RELATIONSHIPS

Relying on intuition can result in good proportional relationships and ultimately adequate color planning. However, there are quantitative measures that can ensure reliable results. "Elements of mass and space have dimensions and, therefore, exist in a mathematical relationship to one another" (Malnar & Vodvarka, 1992, p. 87). Mathematical proportions can be seen in a variety of circumstances—natural forms, the **golden section** (a mathematical formula where an object's width is to its length as its length is to the sum of its length plus width), and the **Fibonacci Sequence** (a series of numbers where each number in the sequence is the sum of the two proceeding numbers). We will examine these theories to establish tools for applying color in proportional amounts later in this chapter. Now, the mention of mathematics may sound a bit daunting. The power of grids for solving complex design problems is limitless. This theory for designing space had long been the practice of many architects and designers. Using grids based on proportional ratios will help you achieve precise proportions and harmony in your work.

Artists such as Piet Mondrian, Robert Mangold, Theo van Doesburg, and Diana Ong have all incorporated grid systems into their art (Figure 6.11). Applying a geometric system can be useful in establishing color relationships.

Charles Rennie Mackintosh (1968–1928) was an architect and designer who studied at the Glasgow School of Art, known for his modern style and innovative work during the Art Nouveau movement. One of his most notable pieces of work is the Hill House, Helensburgh, UK, 1902 to 1903 (Figure 6.12). Mackintosh clearly worked his use of grids into the furnishing of the home. The signature piece, the "Hill House Chair" (right-hand side) illustrates his use of geometric proportions.

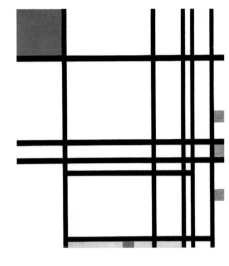

**FIGURE 6.11** Left. *Composition No. 8* by Piet Mondrian, Kimbal Art Museum, Fort Worth, Texas. (© Kimbell Art Museum/Corbis)

**FIGURE 6.12** Bottom. The White Bedroom at Hill House, Helensburgh, by Charles Rennie Macintosh. (© Thomas A. Heinz/Corbis)

**FIGURE 6.13** Right. Color concept diagram. (Courtesy of student Lindsay Perry, University of North Texas.)

**FIGURE 6.14** Bottom. Color grammar in a three-dimensional space. (Courtesy of student Lindsay Perry.)

Terry Knight expresses color and shape in terms of **color grammar**. Much like shape grammar (spatial relationship between various geometric shapes, arrangements, and alignments explore new design language), "in a color grammar the rules and initial shape are defined in terms of lines, labels and *color regions* . . . in two-dimensional color areas or three dimensional color volumes" assigned to specific regions or color spaces in a particular design (1993, p. 119). The grammar produces a series of divisions of a square or other abstract methods such as **Froebel blocks**—a series of wooden stacking blocks in various geometric shapes developed by German Frederick Froebel, who created the concept of kindergarten in the nineteenth century—to study color proportions from color areas versus lines forming shapes that are more closely related to shape/space grammar. For instance, a rectangular form becomes the "vocabulary," two shapes combine in "spatial relation," and when color is applied on the shape, a "color grammar" is created (p. 122). Multiple color grammars can be joined to create a design. In applying this method, you are able to explore color, space, and shape qualitatively.

In Figure 6.13, student Lindsay Perry has applied the concept of color and shape in a conceptual diagram. This diagram serves as the conceptual foundation and color-proportioning system in a two-dimensional format to later be

expanded into a three-dimensional design. This color grammar is one of a series of solutions prepared by the student to explore variations of color and proportional layouts. Once a color/shape grammar has been decided, the student progresses to studying the color proportions and shapes three-dimensionally. Figure 6.14 shows examples of where the color grammar has been applied to a study of vertical path and movement using music and metaphor as the initial determinants for the color grammar. Students are limited to the use of color to explore the intricacies of color that may not otherwise be seen in a scale model. Here, the focus is evenly distributed between color and design.

In Figure 6.15, the concept of shape and color grammar is applied to an additional three-dimensional conceptual study of color, form, and space. In this example, student Christina Masters was assigned the word "flow" as a concept generator. Using this word, the student generated and developed a series of sketches, schematic designs, and finally model prototypes to explore and evaluate the design process. The result is neither an interior nor an exterior but a study of formal relationship of space and order. This project is one of two beginning studies assigned in a course that predominately involves modeling as the primary tool for exploring space. The exercise required the use of white museum board, cardboard, or other lightweight medium versus color to place emphasis on the conceptual design versus materiality and is further restricted to the use of one or two colors integrated with the final design. The intent is to reinforce the individual color connection the student has with the design and how the color is incorporated and supports the final solution. The isolation and added significance of the color in the model makes the exercise challenging and requires the student to think less decoratively about color application. In this example, a contrast of texture using corrugated cardboard and smooth museum board adds interest. The sweeping motion of the design from left to right and back again moves the eye throughout the design for a complete experience. The strong orange color balances nicely with the larger white rectangular forms. The rear portion of the design was elevated to provide a relief and to add further interest with the juxtaposition of positive and negative space.

**FIGURE 6.15** Color grammar in a three-dimensional space. (Courtesy of student Christina Masters, University of Texas.)

Using a grid provides a justification and reasoning behind your color design decisions. Choosing color irrationally or without any research or serious thought can have consequences in your design solutions. Leave the guesswork out when working with color; there are several systems and processes that will make the task less burdensome and overwhelming. When working from photos of interior or images used as inspirational for clients, you can present a preset palette that expresses proportion (before the project is executed in paints, fabrics, and materials and a grand investment is made). This method can be used to train your eye to see color percentages and map out placement, while working with colored media to formulate a color palette and assign colors to objects and areas within a room. Try doing this with several photos on your own and see how you do.

## The Golden Section

The golden section, also known as the golden mean, the golden rectangle, and the golden ratio, developed by the ancient Greeks, is the division of a line in two sections, where the ratio between the smallest section and the largest section is identical to the ratio between the largest section and the entire length of the line (AB is to AC as AC is to CB). "The Golden Section determines a proportion between the whole and its two parts, such that the ratio between the smaller and the larger is the same as the larger and the whole" (Malnar & Vodvarka, 1992, p. 89). This system yields a pleasing proportion of structure and space. The golden section is expressed in the illustration, known as the golden rectangle in Figure 6.16. The most notable example of the golden section is the Parthenon in Athens, Greece, completed in 438 BC.

## Fibonacci Sequence

Leonardo Pisano, more commonly know as Fibonacci, was an Italian mathematician who was born in 1170 and lived during the Renaissance period (Figure 6.17). He is most notable known for having discovered the Fibonacci numbers, a sequence of numbers where each successive number is the sum of the two previous numbers (e.g., 1, 1, 2, 3, 5, 8, 13, 21, 34, 55, 89, 144, and so forth). The higher these number progress in the sequence and divide into one another, the

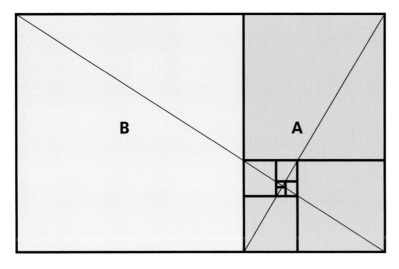

**FIGURE 6.16** The golden rectangle.

closer two numbers next to one another mathematically equals the golden section, which is 1.618. Figure 6.18a illustrates a grid using the Fibonacci Sequence. This grid can be used and expanded to accommodate any proportions that can be applied to initial color planning, as shown in Figure 6.18b.

Nature, as mentioned earlier, tends to organize growth patterns into this sequence. The spiral growth of shells follows the golden spiral, and the golden section is naturally evident; therefore, we automatically judge something in nature as aesthetically pleasing or beautiful. Without the proportion control factor, objects would lack visual appeal and unification. Items such as doors, windows, concrete blocks, and common house brick are example of "manufactured proportions" ensuring that a system is used to maintain consistency and relationship between various architectural design elements (Ching, 1996, p. 282). When you consider that openings and various other elements in an interior correspond to a proportion system or set of rules, and architects commonly work with grid for development of the building shell, it is only logical to consider this same system in your initial color planning. Use these proportions to determine the amount of a color to use. When you identify the formula based on specific laws of proportion, you create a final composition or design that is innately perceived as accurate and sensible. When you choose to work intuitively, the final result may not be as effective. Keep in mind: Color + Proportion = Aesthetic value!

## Le Modulor

Charles Édouard Jeanneret-Gris, who is better known to the design world as Le Corbusier, was a Swiss-born architect who developed the proportioning system, *Le Modulor*, in 1948. Le Corbusier used the golden ratio and Leonardo da Vinci's Vitruvian man (actually created by Vitruvius) to base his system on the human proportions (Figure 6.19). The Modular Man is approximately 6 feet tall, with a raised-arm height of about 7½ feet. The height to the navel is 27½ inches. He took the various points within the human body (ankle height, knee height, waist height, etc.) and devised a series of intervals to be used as a proportioning device based on the golden section ratio. **Anthropometrics** is the study of the average human body dimensions and measurements. These measurements have been

FIGURE 6.17 Right. Portrait of Leonardo Fibonacci. (© Stefano Bianchetti/Corbis)

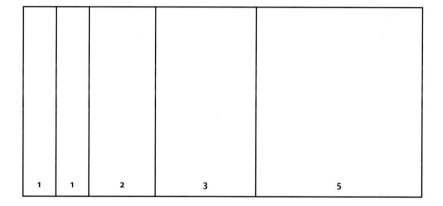

FIGURE 6.18 (a) Top. Grid proportion using the Fibonacci sequence. (b) Bottom. Color palette using the grid from Figure 6.18a.

**FIGURE 6.19** Left. Le Modular: Le Corbusier's *Unite d'habitation*, Marseille.
(© Jack Hobhouse/Alamy)

**FIGURE 6.20** Opposite page. Japanese tatami room. (© Geri Lavrov/Alamy)

used for establishing many of the standardizations of consumer-used products and building design elements.

The golden section developed by the Greeks, Fibonacci Sequence from Italy, and Le Modular from Switzerland goes to illustrate that divine proportions are culturally relative. Modern-day Japan still uses a system based on the traditional tatami mat within the population's residential spaces. The mats are 35.5 by 71 by 2 inches and configured to produce a proportional living space (Figure 6.20). The mats are to be laid in an arrangement where no more than three mats meet at one corner.

Tatami size is said to have been determined by the sleeping area of a person. The introduction of the *shoin-zukuri* style expanded the use of tatami as the entire floor covering over the wooden planks. Tatami became the unit of measure of room size. Many believe that there is just one size of tatami, approximately 6 feet by 3 feet. In fact, there are now three standard sizes depending on geography. Kyoto style tatami are 6.3 feet by 3.1 feet, Nagoya tatami are 6 feet by 3 feet, and Tokyo (Edoma) are 5.8 feet by 2.9 feet. These differences relate to the regional perception of space or lack thereof (Yoshino Japanese Antiques, 1999, pp. 12 and 13).

## Nature's Proportions

Examine various naturally occurring flora and fauna and you can see proportional evolution and growth in natural materials. A prime example of this occurs in the chambers of the nautilus shell (Figure 6.21). Other examples in nature include the spiraling growth patterns of a flowering cactus (Figure 6.22a) or pinecone (Figure 6.22b).

**FIGURE 6.21** Chambered nautilus shell.

(© Lester Lefkowitz/Corbis)

**FIGURE 6.22** (a) Left. Flowering cactus showing proportional growth pattern at Royal Horticultural Society Wisley Garden, Surrey, England. (b) Right. Closeup of pine cone showing proportional growth patterns.

(Left: © Marion Smith/Alamy; right: © David Rowland/Alamy)

**FIGURE 6.23** The Hollyhock House/Aline Barnsdall House, 4808 Hollywood Boulevard, Los Angeles, CA, 1919–1921. Detail of west facade. (© Arcaid/Alamy)

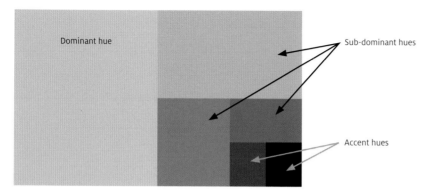

Dominant hue

Sub-dominant hues

Accent hues

**FIGURE 6.24** Variation of a grid for portioning color values.

**FIGURE 6.25** Classical Arne Jacobsen Egg chair in modern loft conversion living room with large window and view of city. (© Elizabeth Whiting & Associates/Alamy)

The basic components of all design are simple shapes—rectangles, circles, squares, and triangles. Frank Lloyd Wright drew inspiration from the hollyhock flower for his design of the 1921 Hollyhock House in Los Angeles, California (Figure 6.23). His refinement of the natural form into basic geometric shapes illustrates the flexibility of nature in creating new forms. If we break color down into the basics for analysis, then application has the potential to be much easier and understandable (Figure 6.24).

The iconic Egg chair designed in 1958 by Arne Jacobsen is an example of the modernistic approach to using simple forms. Jacobsen carved out the desired shape for his chair, creating interplay of positive and negative space while maintaining the simplicity of the original form (Figure 6.25). This same concept is evident in the Ear chair, 1968, by Georges Laporte (Figure 6.26a), and the Tongue chair designed by Pierre Paulin in 1967 (Figure 6.26b). These examples suggest the use of human forms in addition to natural forms for shaping objects into proper proportions.

Examine the color proportions in this closeup view of a butterfly wing in Figure 6.27a. Immediately you can see the accent (blue), a high-intensity hue

**FIGURE 6.26** (a) Top. Ear chair by Georges Laporte, 1968. High-color contrast between inside and outside forms highlight this chair's design features. (b) Right. Tongue chair by Pierre Paulin, 1967. The whimsical design of this chair is accentuated using bright, saturated hues for the upholstery.

(Top: CHRISTIE'S IMAGES LTD., 2009; right: Artifort)

**FIGURE 6.27** (a) Top. Thousands of tiny, colored scales create a mosaic pattern on the wing of a butterfly. (b) Left. Butterfly wing color proportioned into a palette using the grid format. (Top: © Laura Sivell; Papilio/Corbis)

in the mix that receives the smallest proportion. This is followed by three other colors with identifiable proportions that we can apply to a grid for comparison, as shown in Figure 6.27b.

Nature informs design. Recall from Chapter 4 that analyzing nature's color assists in establishing good proportional rhythm. These proportions can therefore be broken down into increments using a grid system based on the golden section or Fibonacci Sequence. Using nature as a source for inspiration and creativity allows for your design to develop more fluidly. Students are exposed to alternative forms for exploring design and therefore retain a greater awareness through observation and exploration of uncommon forms and color patterns, tapping into the beauty of nature and its potential to influence color design decisions.

It is only natural that we consider proportion and color. The visible spectrum itself is separated into wavelengths of difference proportions and lengths, innately informing us that the basis for color itself is a proportionate measure. Color by proportion seeks a completeness and aesthetic value. When designers communicate color with the principles, we create a new design process for exploring the use of colors. In doing so we have opened up an opportunity to express new ideas and design concepts as well as to establish the foundation for future perspectives and creative approaches to interior design. Design is approached using the elements and principles to find the right balance of creativity and function while introducing style and aesthetic value. Don't be afraid to experiment with color. According to Galen Cranz, "The implicit theory is that the design line, proportions, shapes, and decorative motifs of the time crystallize the concerns and aspirations of the day" (2000, p. 11).

## KEY WORDS

Proportion, scale, golden section, color grammar, Fibonacci Sequence, Froebel blocks, Le Modular, anthropometrics

# color + proportion + scale

## LEARNING OUTCOMES

- Proportions of color should be considered in the context of the scale of the space and amount of lighting available.
- Using a grid system based on the golden section, Fibonacci, Le Modular, or natural forms can provide a more accurate method for establishing relative color proportions in the initial planning stages of your design projects.
- Scale and proportion can enhance and alter the visual perception of our environment.
- Scale refers to our relationship of the human body to objects, whereas proportion refers to the size and arrangement of objects with each other in an interior space.
- Natural color forms can be identified for establishing relative proportions and can then be translated into interior projects.
- Using shape grammar with three-dimensional studies opens a window for exploring the color proportions in the built environment.

## EXERCISES

1. Using the proportional systems discussed in the chapter, develop a color composition using 1 to 5 colors varying in value and intensity. Next, develop a second composition that reverses the assigned proportions to see the change that occurs in the perception of the overall scheme. Develop a 1- to 2-paragraph analysis of what occurs with the color reversal. Exchange designs (but not analyses) with a classmate analyze one another's compositions in 1 or 2 paragraphs. Compare your own analyses with the classmate's analyses. Where did your opinions and impressions overlap, and where did they differ?

2. Locate a photo of a quality designed interior from a credible design publication. The photo can be any type of interior (retail, hospitality, healthcare, residential, office, and more). Using colored papers and the image; develop an abstract collage composition of color proportion base on variations of the color scheme within the photo. Mount your design onto illustration board or other sturdy recyclable artist board. Do not duplicate the shapes or recreate the image. Provide a written analysis of how the collage relates in proportion and scale to the magazine clipping. Document and provide credit to the magazine, page number, and designer (if available) for the photo chosen. The purpose is to emulate (1) the color palette, (2) the proportions, and (3) the essence of the photo

3. Locate a multicolored (neutral or colored) natural object such as a sea shell, leaf, flower, pine cone, or a photo of a colorful fish, bird, or butterfly. Using any colored media of your choosing, create a composition of colors with proportions the same as those within the natural object. This exercise tests your ability to identify color proportion, and also tests your ability to correctly select colored media that accurately mirrors the colors in the natural object.

color +
unity +
harmony

Color is the personality of each design element chosen for an interior. Before we can touch an object, we see it, and in that moment, the color and object communicate. The color combination in any design can attract attention, establish meaning, and provide beauty. **Unity** is defined as the repetition of color to achieve a unified whole. **Harmony** is the result of a perfect balance between individual color relationships. A color harmony can be recognized when our eyes are not overworked when trying to view the scheme. If the color combinations result in a pleasing whole where no one color stands out, then you've achieved a color harmony. "Our brains look for elements, and when we recognize them we see a cohesive design rather than unorganized chaos" (Lauer & Pentak, 2007, p. 29).

Unity and harmony of space can be achieved through similarity of color, shape, and form. Color, shape, and form are inseparable design elements. Individually, shape and color may be perceived as being modified in appearance due to their surroundings or by the angle in which they are viewed; separate they are unpredictable, together they are much stronger. Without unity there is no harmony. Color harmony suggests "that color cannot be separated from one another" and that "form strengthens color and vice versa" (Burchett, 2005, p. 50). For instance, when a round button on a computer is accented with the hue red, the button communicates what the object is, and it is color that allows the eye to discern its purpose: Power OFF. "A literal application of this theory might lead to the conclusion that color produces an essentially emotional experience, whereas shape corresponds to the intellectual control" (Arnheim, 1974, p. 336). A careful balancing of the emotional and visual stimuli will result in unity and harmonizing of interior spaces.

Achieving visual harmony varies with the systems being used. What might look right in the red, yellow, blue (RYB) pigment system may not look the same using CMYK process system. Therefore, variation of color harmonies will be dictated by the source. For our purposes, we will use the standard RYB, which is more common among artists and paint manufacturers. The work of most designers will eventually move beyond traditional color harmonies to exploring more dynamic and innovative approaches to color use. Now it is time to learn the basics of color harmonizing and those colors that work well together and those

that do not. Color changes as fashions and trends change, and a color that is widely received today could be shunned tomorrow. During the 1970s the colors avocado green and harvest gold were fashionable for home interiors, followed by mauve and country blue in the 1980s, and burgundy and hunter green in the 1990s. Cultural movements produce changes in color preferences, which also influence color decisions (explained further in Chapter 9); however, we must be careful not to be too prescriptive about color harmony, lest we forget that it rests partly in theory and partly as a matter of personal preference.

There is no one ideal way for identifying and selecting harmonious color schemes. Regardless of whether you know anything about color harmony, one can see when a color combination is in **discord**—that is, a loosely organized, disharmonized combination that departs from the natural ordering of color. The harmonies described below will hopefully lead you to explore other variations of color pairings, intensity levels, and values shifts. Today, a wide variety of color palettes are generated in the marketplace and constantly evolve to fill the needs of consumer tastes. As long as theory is used as a general guide and the tendency is suppressed to impart your own subjective and personal attributes to a particular project, the opportunities for creating interesting color palettes are endless. The importance of getting to know your client should not be understated.

## SIX ELEMENTS OF COLOR HARMONY

Birren identified six elements to of color harmony based on the original research conducted in 1839 by Chevreul. In Birren's book, *Principles of Color* (1969, pp. 34–35), harmonies of analogy and harmonies of contrast are identified.

1. "The harmony of scale in which closely related values of a single hue are exhibited together."
2. "The harmony of hues in which analogous colors of similar value are exhibited."
3. "The harmony of a dominant colored light in which an assortment of different hues and values is pervaded as if by a dominant tinted light."
4. "The harmony of contrast of scale in which strongly different values of a single hue are combined."

5. "The harmony of contrast of hues in which related colors are exhibited in strongly different values (and strongly different degrees of purity or chroma)."

6. "The harmony of contrast of colors . . . colors belonging to scales very far asunder"—in other words, colors that are separated or that are farther apart from one another on the color wheel (red and green, blue-green and red-orange). The farther apart hues are located on the color wheel, the higher the contrast. Contrasts between hues ultimately add visual rhythm and variety into a space. Colors closer together have a softer contrast, while colors farther apart have a harder and stronger visual contrast.

## Harmonies of Analogy

Adjacent hues on the color wheel have lesser contrast but also will come together in palettes that are either warm (red, red-orange, yellow-orange) or cool (blue, blue-green, green). A palette could include both warm and cool hues (blue, blue-violet, red-violet). The inclusion of warm and cool hues adds to color harmony. Below are some types of harmony that designers try to achieve:

The closer the hues lay together on the color wheel, the lower the apparent contrast will be within an interior space. Creating analogous schemes that incorporate both warm and cool hues will increase the contrast level; however, contrast is moderate because they are relatively close or adjacent to each other on the color wheel.

## Harmonies of Contrast

Color opposites on the color wheel create the most vivid contrasts. These schemes are used whenever visual impact is required. This color harmony is effective for retail and hospitality spaces associated with activity, excitement, and energy.

## THE SEVEN COLOR HARMONIES

Harmony in color is beauty in nature; the color compositions seem natural as if plucked from the ground where no one color battles for dominance nor does one color stand out in the crowd. Harmony is totality, a palette that is seen as one versus many. When your eyes analyze a color palette and you get a sense or feeling that all is correct, your intuition is telling you the color arrangement is harmonious. For some, the intuitive skill requires refinement; for others, it comes naturally. However, good intuition does not rule out the need to understand the color relationships that for many a decade theorists have studied and written about.

Color harmony can be achieved through similarity in the color choices made for an interior space. The principle of **uniform connectedness** suggests that "elements that are connected by uniform visual properties, such as color, are perceived to be more related than elements that are not connected" (Lidwell, Holden, & Butler, 2003, p. 200). When all the elements and principles of design work in tandem, a natural organization of space occurs. When interior design elements do not share a basic visual language, a recognizable pattern is required to better understand the relationship of the parts to the whole. One way this can be done within your home involves a room setting where you wish to group together a variety of photos (places, people, landscapes, contemporary, traditional) that share no common visual language in one location within an interior space. If you group each of these photos with frames in a similar color and style, the collection will appear to relate, now that they have a common organizational design feature. With this method, you have unified the different photos and created harmony of the collection. Color harmony is critical when you consider that a space can be combined of many different materials (wall covering, paint, carpets, wood, fabrics, and decorative elements) in different quantities. The interior design must relate these interior features using the appropriate color (hue), for the space, the right balance of values (lights and darks) to add depth and articulation of design features, and lastly, chroma (bright and dull) to add drama and visual interest to create personality and purpose for the space in use.

Colors perception differs from person to person. Particular color "personalities" come forth as a result of individual differences in hue, value, and saturation levels. Depending on these levels, certain color personalities harmonize well together and others do not. When too many colors are combined with too many variations in value and saturation level, the result can be chaotic and lack unity. On the other extreme, if too much of the same color is used extensively throughout a space, the interior becomes uninteresting. "Variety, on the other hand, when

carried to an extreme for the sake of interest, can result in visual chaos . . . it is the careful and artistic tension between order and disorder, between unity and variety that enlivens harmony and creates interest in an interior setting" (Ching & Binggeli, 2005, p. 136).

It is important to understand the difference between a color "harmony" and a color "scheme." A scheme is a plan for a design. Often what we plan for a space isn't always the best solution. Interior designers are confronted on occasion with color schemes prepared by other sources, oftentimes retailers of fabrics, paints, wall coverings, and so forth. In most of these cases, the schemes are well prepared, and in other times, they need reworking to be effective for your particular design. In the latter, you are seeking a "harmony" for an outcome that works well and is desirable by you and your clients. Here we will discuss the theory for specific harmonies that can be applied when selecting colors for a particular scheme.

There are seven types of color harmonies: monochromatic, complementary, split complementary, analogous, triadic, tetrad, and multi-hued schemes. In Chapter 1 we defined the basic color harmonies most interior design practitioners utilize in their work. Of these seven types, two are more practically usable and easier to work with: complementary (contrast) scheme and analogous (gradation of hue, not chroma).

## Monochromatic

Monochromatic is the easiest harmony to identify and work with. A single hue is selected with variations in tint, tones, and shades to provide variety in the palette (Figure 7.1a). This palette is very simple and easy to recognize partially due to the absence of or limited high contrasts. To prevent this scheme from being monotonous, the use of textures and value contrasts is important in creating visual interest in the space (Figure 7.1b). In addition, without enough visual contrast, the space can be confusing and potentially add to safety concerns if changes in floor and other surfaces levels are not easily identifiable. In Figure 7.2, the abundant use of the same value of red can be disorienting, and therefore, safety is an issue when a person is attempting to use the staircase. This is a prime example of how color has the potential to impact the health, safety, and welfare of anyone, even

**FIGURE 7.1** (a) Right. Monochromatic color harmony. (b) Bottom. Monochromatic interior color scheme. (Bottom: © Pieter Estersohn/Beateworks/Corbis)

more so someone with compromised vision, such as an older adult. Imagine this in a large-scale commercial space versus a small residential space. The negative outcomes would be severe.

In Figure 7.3, the opposite is true of the monotony theory. This interior of the Blue Lounge at the Camino Real Hotel in Mexico City uses a highly saturated blue that is meant to relax visitors in the lounge area. Sound from the pool of water, horizontal lines of the architectural elements on the far wall, and low color contrast all lead to the desired outcome.

In Figure 7.4, the large gathering space is predominantly one shade of blue; however, the space works for two different reasons: (1) There is a good balance between textural surfaces and contrast of light and dark materials, and (2) the wood flooring casts a yellow-orange hue complementing the blue. Materials, fabrics, and paints all work to create a color harmony.

**FIGURE 7.2** Top. Potential safety hazard: View of an entryway from the staircase in saturated red tones where level changes are not distinguished well. (© Tim Street-Porter/Beateworks/Corbis)

**FIGURE 7.3** Right. The Blue Lounge at the Camino Real Hotel in Mexico City. (© Franz-Marc Frei/Corbis)

**FIGURE 7.4** Opposite page. Monochromatic with complementary tones in wood floor accent this side view of a huge hall that consists of a sofa set and a conference table.

(© Pieter Estersohn/Beateworks/Corbis)

## Complementary

Complementary color palettes (Figure 7.5) are often chosen for their visual interest, their high contrast, and their ability to accent the interior with a dominant hue. These colors schemes usually include one cool and one warm hue, which create the vivid contrasts (Figure 7.6a) and high energy associated with complements. Varying the degree of lightness (tint) and/or darkness (shade) of one of the complementary hues will minimize this effect (Figure 7.6b). Figure 7.6c illustrates a concept of opposing colors overlapping one another to show the brilliance, purity, and contrast level that can be achieved with complementary harmonies. You will notice that in each of these three illustrations, varying the amounts of each color will create a more pleasing harmony. With each color harmony, you do not have to have equal amounts of each color. Too consistent amounts of each color could result in monotony. Light color can balance the dark, and the dark colors could provide visual relief from intense colors. For each of these harmonies, a careful balance of light and dark, high and low saturation is achieved.

## Split Complementary and Double Complementary

Split complements (Figure 7.7) are much in the same; rather than taking the opposite color from the starting hue on the color wheel, you select the two colors on either side of its complement. This scheme has less visual contrast than a direct complement but adds the third color to give you more variety in your color planning. Double-split complementary includes two adjacent hues and their complements (Figure 7.8). As with any scheme, proportioning is the key to making it successful. Refer to the strategies outlined in Chapter 6.

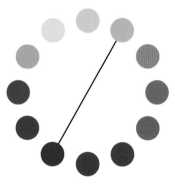

**FIGURE 7.5** Complementary color harmony.

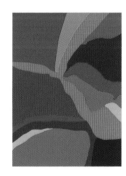

**FIGURE 7.6** (a) Left. Itten's contrast of warm and cool. (b) Middle. Itten's contrast of tint and shade. (c) Right. Itten's contrast of complements. (Images courtesy of http://www.worqx.com © Janet Lynn Ford, 1998.)

119

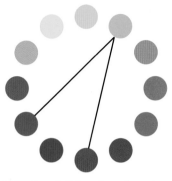

**FIGURE 7.7** Split Complementary color

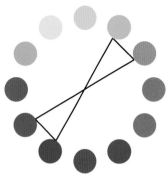

**FIGURE 7.8** Double-split Complementary color

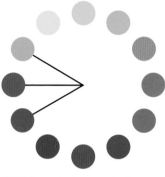

**FIGURE 7.9** Analogous color harmony.

FIGURE 7.10 This red kitchen lacks visual contrast to harmonize and provide the needed visual relief. (© Patrik Engquist/Etsa/Corbis)

## Analogous

Analogous schemes, which incorporate between three and five adjacent hues, allow a designer to vary color while still maintaining a recognizable relationship (Figure 7.9). An analogous scheme, with its absence of a strong complement, makes the color schemes less startling and more inviting. This scheme might be used in a space where people want to feel calm and relieved of anxiety, or when extended periods of stay may occur, such as in hospital waiting rooms, restaurants for fine dining, living and conversation spaces, and places for rest and sleeping. Choose an analogous scheme that incorporates at least 50 percent of the hues from the cool side of the color wheel. Analogous color schemes will have one parent hue that is repeated in at least two-thirds of the total composition (red, red-orange, orange or blue, blue-green, green). In Figure 7.10, a kitchen with red cabinets, a red table, and modern orange lamp lacks the harmony needed to make the space pleasing. The red is overpowering and needs an additional, lighter analogous hue in yellow or a shift to a yellow-green accent to maintain the analogous scheme but introduce the underlying complement, green, to soften the abundant use of red. Any one of the colors within the analogous scheme can be used as the dominant color, or the colors can be equally distributed in the space; in any situation, analogous color harmonies provide great flexibility.

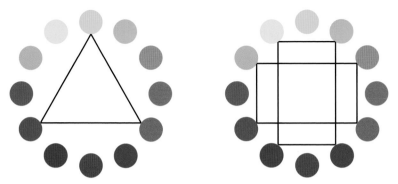

**FIGURE 7.11** (a) Left. Triadic color harmony. (b) Right. Tetrad color harmony.

## Triadic and Tetrad

Triadic color harmonies include three colors that are equidistant from one another, and tetrad includes four equally spaced colors on the color wheel. Much like the complement harmony, triadic and tetrad offer obvious contrast and result

in palettes that are predominately warm or cool depending on the location of the scheme within the color wheel (Figure 7.11b). With three colors opposing one another and vying for dominance, this scheme must establish one of the hues as the dominant proportion, with the remaining two taking on subdominant roles Figures 7.12a and 7.12b are interior examples of triadic and tetrad color harmonies, respectively.

In Figure 7.12a, the triadic harmony of purple, orange, and green has been applied. In this kitchen space, the orange hue is represented in the natural color from the wood flooring and cabinetry, green accented in the solid-surface countertop for the bar area, and the dominant purple hue for the interior wall surfaces. In Figure 7.12b, the color scheme has been modified to include a tetrad scheme of two complementary schemes—blue and orange and red and green. The colors' intensities were modified for harmony resulting in the following assigned colors: peach (birch wood cabinets), steel-blue (stainless-steel blue countertops and appliances), chartreuse (wall color), and deep red (barstools). Establishing dominance and proportions is a key to making this successful. Much like the

**FIGURE 7.12** (a) Left. Interior example of a triadic color harmony. (b) Middle. Interior example of a tetrad color harmony. (c) Right. Original kitchen interior before color harmonies were assigned. (Illustrations by Steven Stankiewicz)

complementary color schemes, the nature of triadic and tetrad color schemes equidistant across the color wheel creates dynamic and attention-grabbing harmony. Figure 7.12c is the original illustration for comparison of the effects with the spaces from the interior color harmony manipulations.

## Multi-hue

The last of the schemes to be discussed is the multi-hue color scheme. This scheme appears to suggest that all rules are out—pick whatever and however many colors you want. On the contrary, this scheme is the most difficult to use because it is entirely dependent on the proportions of the colors to achieve the right harmony. Two keys concepts have to be considered. First, you need to establish a relationship within the palette between all colors—for instance, in the series of blue, blue-green, red-orange, and red. Because of shared hues, they are all complementary to one another. You can insert an accent—in this case yellow—and you have a five-part color harmony. Second, you need to properly proportion the colors to balance the mix. A dominant hue will need to be identified that will be the obvious color emphasized within the space. Figure 7.13 illustrates the 12-step color wheel and the colors proportioned into a palette of multi-hue color harmony. If

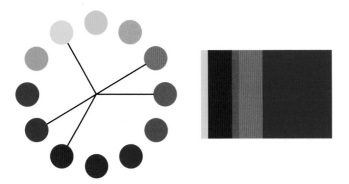

**FIGURE 7.13** Multi-hue color harmony.

you refer back to Figure 5.7, you can see an example of multicolor harmony. The blue is used as the dominant hue to unite the columns and harmonize the space. Figure 7.14 provides a chart for monochromatic, analogous, triadic, and complementary color harmonies in an expanded color range of all 12 hues in the basic color circle. This can be used when you are making decisions about particular color harmonies in your projects.

## Achromatic

Achromatic or color-neutral schemes are popular in many residential interiors because of the simplicity and focus on natural color, devoid of manufactured processes that add the color pigment. These schemes are usually based around colors such as gray, ivory, tan, brown, khaki, beige, black, and white. In most cases, such schemes are intended to focus on the physical characteristics of the interior and materials used in the design of the space. Philip Johnson's Glass House, built from 1948 to 1949 in New Canaan, Connecticut, is an exemplary use of natural materials and an open plan, with the large, light-glazed area blurring the lines between inside and outside (Figure 7.15). In this setting, the use of colored hues would be out of place. To prevent monotony, add light and dark value contrasts of the neutral scheme, vary the lighting sources between both natural and artificial, and vary the textures to harmonize an achromatic color scheme. In Figure 7.16, the large red rug adds an accent color to the otherwise achromatic color scheme. The interior has been designed with high contrasts of values from light to dark, various textures (rough and smooth), and a variety of materials (glass, wood, and textiles), all harmonizing with clean, simple lines allowing the strong red to brighten the dark floor and take its place as the focal point. The addition of an accent color is sometimes used in achromatic schemes to add more visual interest.

## Color, Space, Harmony

The fear of using bright color might be called in Latin "mega-pigmento-chromophobia" (Lehndorff, 2002, p. 1E). The tendency and sage advice has historically

# color + unity + harmony

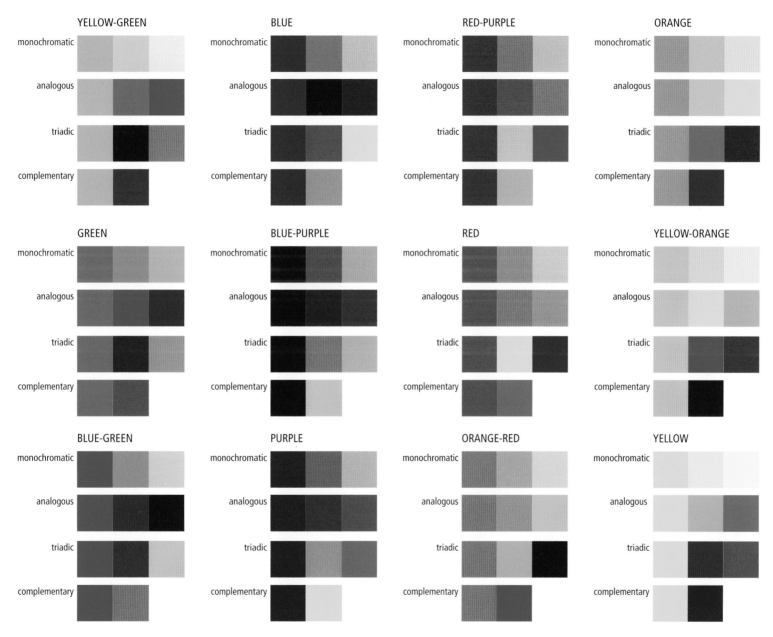

**FIGURE 7.14** Twelve-hue color harmony chart. (Image provided courtesy of Claritas Consortium design group, Portland, Oregon, www.claritasconsortium.com.)

**FIGURE 7.15** Top. Barcelona daybed and chairs in Glass House. (© Bill Maris/Arcaid/Corbis)

**FIGURE 7.16** Right. Lobby at the Metropolitan Hotel in Bangkok. (© Luca Tettoni/Corbis)

been to stick with safe, neutral tones that won't make a splash. People who are simply untrained in the methods for applying color principles may suffer from indecision at crucial moments in the planning process—the conceptualization and application of color to a room's design elements. Many a client has lived in spaces with poor color harmonies only never to realize that the source of the problem *was* color.

"Excessive unity is often the pitfall of the beginning designer who, in an effort to keep control over the design, limits the visual palette too much…the best design is actually varied and subtly complex; it does not reduce the problem to its simplest terms, yet remains controlled" (Faimon & Weigand, 2004, p. 29). In Figure 7.17a, the interior of this hospital waiting room has been excessively limited in color. In addition, the single hue (blue) has been overused, creating a lifeless interior. Dark and highly saturated deep blue, a cold hue, is often perceived as depressive. Blue in this interior can produce a calming affect, suitable for a hospital waiting space, where anxiety and emotions can run high; however, this particular hue is too brash and not suitable for this particular application. Alone, the subtle use of violet for the guest chairs isn't enough of an analogous shift to circumvent the solemn character of the space. Often we think that cool, calming hues are the only option for relaxing or reducing nervous tension, but it is the use of saturation that can bring about the same results without relying solely on cool or analogous hues. If we (1) introduce an extended palette of colors, (2) reduce the intensity of those hues, and (3) create a contrast of hues, attention is drawn to architectural details such as moldings, columns, and the nurses' station. These areas "pop" in contrast to the original space and now have more visual interest and still maintain a soft, warm, welcoming space. The high contrast assigned to the crown molding serves to introduce rhythm and carry the eye around the room's perimeter without being overwhelming (Figure 7.17b). By introducing contrasting hues (adobe red and sage green) that are lowered in chroma, the color plan begins to harmonize and unify the furnishings and accessories. Additionally, hues in soft blue-greens and golden-wheat complement and extend the finished interior.

**FIGURE 7.17a** The character of this hospital waiting room can be perceived as solemn and depressing when the wrong hue and intensity are used. (Illustration by Steven Stankiewicz)

**FIGURE 7.17b** Introducing color harmony with complements red and green, light and dark contrasts, and fabric patterns; the interior of this waiting room is welcoming and cheerful. (Illustration by Steven Stankiewicz)

Figure 7.18 illustrates a small sampling of color schemes based on current trends in the home furnishings industry; these combinations would have seemed out of place 10 to 15 years ago. The palettes are more exotic and vibrant than in previous years. Color in the retail industry changes swiftly, and period palettes and those associated with particular design movements may inspire your interior color schemes. When working in period styles, research the colors for accuracy—this is an additional source for color inspiration and harmonious palettes that are timeless. The *Color Compendium* by Hope and Walch (1990) is an excellent source for historical and cultural color harmonies. In Figures 7.19a to 7.19c, students generate a color study of historical palettes shaped into various motifs from the art deco period.

**FIGURE 7.18** Four examples of color trends using the grid. Driven by social, cultural, environmental, and political changes, color trends are identified by multiple influences from around the world and are becoming more playful, eco-inspired, and representative of our global uniqueness.

(a) Art deco. (Courtesy of Charli Winston, Chuck Reed, Kathleen Shelton, and Kameron Thomas.)

(b) Art nouveau. (Courtesy of Ryan Young, Vita Palmeri, and Bamma King.)

(c) Arts & Crafts. (Courtesy of Jessie Dodd, Kristen Dow, and Lee Francis.)

**FIGURE 7.19** Historical color palettes.

When working out various color harmonies, consider the surface background you are using, because this will affect the color harmony. We know that no color is isolated and thus colors affect one another. A blue-green hue next to a blue hue will appear greener than when next to a green hue. A white or black background will alter the lightness or darkness of a color; therefore, it is recommended that work be based on a neutral light gray, which will have the least visual impact on the color harmony. Figure 7.20 illustrates this concept. A single palette could look dramatically different with changes in background surface.

Many theoretical approaches to understanding color harmony have been developed for artists, interior designers, graphic designers, and architects in an effort to help them make sound color choices. If you like color, do not deprive yourself of the joy in using it in your own space or in design projects for others. Many factors, including natural and artificial light, will soften intense colors, and remember that larger area of lighter colors may appear darker or more intense when selected from small color charts.

## KEY WORDS

Unity, harmony, discord, monochromatic, complementary, split complementary, double complementary, analogous, triad, tetrad, multi-hue, achromatic, uniform connectedness

## LEARNING OUTCOMES

- Colors that share a common hue will relate and harmonize better than colors that have no common color connection.
- Repetition of color throughout a space unifies the palette and the interior design.
- One color can be used to unify two different design elements.
- Color gradation of value and intensity can be used to distinguish between two similar design elements.
- Uniform distribution and use of color in a complex interior space can harmonize the visual clutter.
- Color harmonies should be planned to accentuate the interior, not overwhelm the space.

## EXERCISES

1. Create a 12-step color wheel using Color-aid or other forms of colored media. This tool will be used in developing color harmonies. While purchasing a color wheel is an option and less of a time commitment, the act of creating the wheel will teach you about the relationship of various hues and their placement along the wheel.

2. Create a monochromatic color harmony with a minimum of three values.

3. Create two analogous color harmonies (one keyed to red and one keyed to blue).

4. Create three complementary color harmonies (one with each major hue, red, blue, green).

5. Create a split-complementary color harmony using violet as your dominant hue.

6. Create a triad color harmony.

7. Create a tetrad color harmony.

8. Create a multi-hue color harmony, paying attention to proportion and keyed to a dominant hue for unity in the composition. Use a minimum of five hues.

9. Select a piece of art from an art catalog. Use this art to create a color board based on the color harmony in the artwork. Select the interior finish materials such as wall paint, trim, flooring, and four textiles (for sofa, chair, drapery, and accent) to convey the essence of the art.

10. Create a discord harmony using three to four colors. Using the same parent hue for each color chosen in the discord, select three to four new colors, varying only the original color's value or saturation to bring the discord into harmony. Compare the two harmonies, and analyze the steps taken to correct the discord.

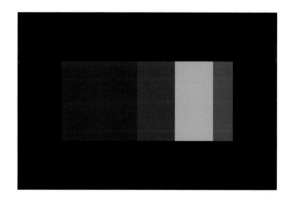

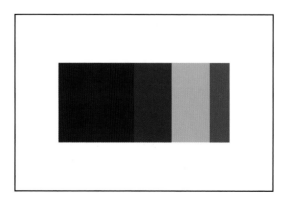

**FIGURE 7.20** Color palettes alter when viewed on different background surfaces—simultaneous contrast.

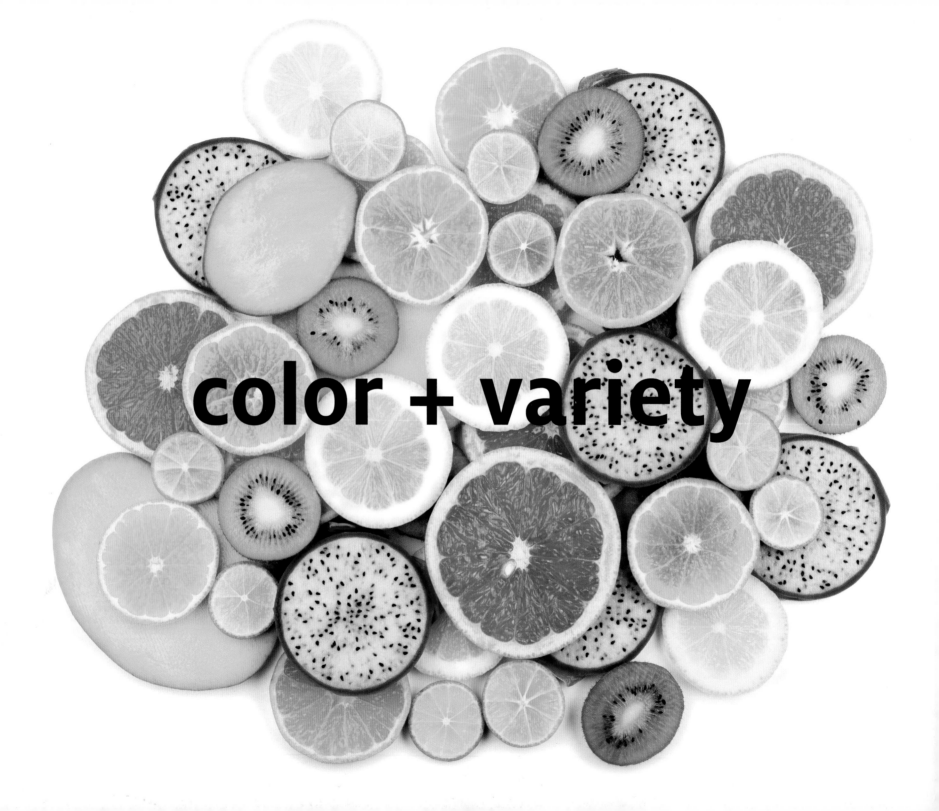
color + variety

8

In order to understand how color is to be used beautifully, to add interest and excitement to a space, it is necessary to look at variety as one of the key principles of design to achieve this end. It is essential to train color judgment, to build confidence in using color, and to learn color use with the right amount of fact and knowledge combined with intuition. After reading this book and completing the exercises, you should be able to invent many stimulating color solutions for your interior design projects.

"Order without diversity can result in monotony or boredom, diversity without order can produce chaos . . . A sense of unity with variety is the ideal" (Ching, 1996, p. 320). **Variety** is the principle of design that is concerned with the combination of one or more color elements with shape, form, pattern, and texture to create diversity and contrast in an interior space. Without color variety, a space is static and inactive, and lacks the particular design effect to make the visual composition interesting. "Design implies a plan, a conscious intent. When an image becomes too complex, whether by intention or by accident—when too much variety becomes visually chaotic—the image ceases to be designed . . . design implies some amount of control" (Faimon & Weigand, 2004, p. 27). It is simple: Don't decorate. The lack of control shows a lack of skill and will be evident to your clients.

A balance of visual dullness and visual variety is necessary to prevent an overly animated space. Kopacz states in *Color for Three-Dimensional Design:* " . . . an overabundance of complexity may over-stimulate the occupant to the point of stress, evidenced by changes in pulse rate, blood pressure, or breathing" (2004, p. 68).

Early in this book we discussed the power of using a grid to prepare proportional relationships among colors. When seeking to unify a variety of objects, using a grid is a way to organize the potential chaos into a system that allows for the variation of design elements to be viewed as a whole. This method is a great way to organize a personal collection. Too many times, clients' spaces are cluttered with a scattering of objects collected from travels or personal collections they've accumulated over the years. At some point, the collection reaches a size that requires a design plan that establishes order, using one or two as a focal point, or perhaps editing the collection. The colored glass vase collection

**FIGURE 8.1** Variety of color and shape are illustrated in this collection of glass vases and bowls organized within white casework. (© Tim Street-Porter/Beateworks/Corbis)

in Figure 8.1 becomes a focal wall organized into the white cabinet (grid) where variety and unity integrate in a workable solution.

## VARIETY AND INTEREST

A color scheme can enhance the visual interest of your interior space. Selecting one or more hues from a color wheel and varying the lightness or darkness of the chosen color allows variety and interest to form. As you are selecting hues, keep in mind that using values—black, white, and gray (achromatic)—are just as visually active as colored hues (Figure 8.2). Use colors to explain your design, not decorate. If you use color purely for decorative means, the final design could show compromised quality. The physical design of a particular space—the layout, interior architectural features, lighting design, hardware, and textiles, to name a few elements—should be supported by the colors you agree on with partners and clients. Color applied decoratively doesn't consider the design, its intended purpose, and the way the user is to respond and interact with the design. For instance, using a dark, dull color at an interior entrance might give the signal "stay away" or "private," thus contradicting the motive to enter through a clear entrance and stay in an inviting space. This color choice could obscure the entrance and hide or distract from the design's purpose. On the contrary, an entrance that is dark but contrasted with lighter surroundings within will add variety and interest, stand out, and therefore draw attention and provide "identity and hierarchy" (Ching, 1996, p. 108). The color and contexts of its use should be considered for the final design to be successful; color as decoration may not guarantee success.

Variety adds the visual break from a design, much like emphasis, but in a more complex manner. Variety focuses on more than one object, clustered in a composition sharing similar traits such as size, shape, or pattern. Use color, or similar color values, and saturation to group design elements or concepts and establish correlations within your design. In Figure 8.3, the lobby ceiling in the Bellagio Hotel, Las Vegas, is covered with colored, amoeba-like glass forms by Dale Chihuly. The variety of color adds the drama and interest, while the cluster application is a unified whole.

**FIGURE 8.2** A modern living space using achromatic color contrasts for added variety.
(© Fancy/Veer/Corbis)

Variety introduces a different character to an element for the purpose of creating contrast that in turn creates interest. Unity, as discussed in Chapter 7, limits disorganization and "decorative" novelty, while variety generates contrast and visual interest. The two design principles are interconnected; however, unity and harmony must dominate if the interior space is to work as a whole unit. Unity must also be balanced by some variety, or the interior space will be too boring. Variety occurs through contrast. Contrast in design elements can be a device to hold the attention of the viewer and create a visually stimulating interior. **Contrast**—or the juxtaposition of different forms, lines, or colors in a space "to intensify each element's properties and produce a more dynamic expressiveness"—especially if it is unusual, is often the feature that earns the most attention (Ching, 1996, p. 380). The red lounge in Figure 8.4 contrasts with the neutral palette of materials and finishes in this modern bedroom space. These contrasting design principles help prevent boredom and loss of interest.

Visual differentiation among objects, surfaces, planes, foreground, and background not only aids in communicating your design intent but adds the visual

**FIGURE 8.3** Top. Glass ceiling sculpture entitled *Fiore di Como* by Dale Chihuly breaks the monotony of a white ceiling in the lobby of the Bellagio Hotel and Casino, Las Vegas. (© Blaine Harrington III/Corbis)

**FIGURE 8.4** Right. Various sizes, different shapes, colors, textures, and patterns combine to accentuate and add interest in this modern bedroom space. (© Andrew Twort/Alamy)

**FIGURE 8.5a** This residential dining space requires variety through color and pattern to accentuate the interior and further define the eating area. (Illustration by Steven Stankiewicz)

**FIGURE 8.5b** A complementary color scheme of blue-green and orange enlivens this dining space with added elements to define and strengthen the interior design. (Illustration by Steven Stankiewicz)

texture and movement necessary to form unity and harmony. In Figure 8.5a, the dining room necessitates color variety and definition of spatial elements to clarify and unify the design. Without color and pattern, the space loses the distinction necessary for a user to appreciate the furnishings and define the space for dining. The wall at the end of the dining table can be accented and serve as a design feature. Applying square-shaped mirrors with the negative space painted in the orange hue of the chairs creates needed variety and pattern. The physical dining space is further defined by a wood floor inlay to offset this zone and mimic the ceiling design. This carries the wood finish throughout the interior (Figure 8.5b).

Use color to establish a variety of textures, patterns, and visual expectations from your design plan. Patterns, when used consistently, can unify one or multiple adjoining spaces. Once you have established a color plan, it's imperative you stick to it. If you choose to depart from your design plan and use a different set of color patterns within a single space, do so only to emphasize a particular design element. You can encourage the emphasis by using a hue with a higher saturation level or high-contrast colors to attract attention to major design features in your space. With an open floor plan, the tendency is to change color pattern and hue within separate activity areas. Be cautious not to add variety that will not unify with the other adjoining spaces. When changing hues, stay with similar values and intensities to avoid adding visual clutter. Remember: Less is more. By limiting your use of color, you will maximize its impact on the overall design. In Figure 8.6, the interior waiting room and reception area of the space uses simple lines and neutral-colored interior finishes. To add contrast and variety, the orange circles positioned above within glass gradually increase in size, also adding visual texture and interest for a clean, simple, modern space.

To the contrary, a colorless space can appear dismal and uninviting. Consider the space in Figure 8.7a. A restaurant should be a place of socialization and celebration. Color is key to setting a particular mood and theme for spaces of

**FIGURE 8.6** Colored circles add visual variety and interest to a simple reception/waiting area.

(© Peter Durant/Arcaid/Corbis)

entertainment. For example, in a fine-dining, restaurant, colors may be reduced in intensity and darker to increase the desire to linger, whereas in a fast-food restaurant, bright colors give the perception of quick service. In the figure, the large window wall provides ample natural light, giving the space the option of being darkened for an intimate dining experience. The curvilinear design elements do not receive importance or separation from other materials through value contrast. The open kitchen concept, a common point of focus in a restaurant, blends in with the surroundings. This spatial composition needs variety through added color contrast that will unify and strengthen the design. Introducing a greater degree of contrasts assigned to key elements (ceiling, rear accent wall, and open kitchen) creates added variety in the restaurant to stimulate patron's experience of place. The changes in Figure 8.7b provide the visual contrast and variety necessary to the layout.

Design planes (columns, walls, and ceilings) can each be enhanced with color to add more variety. No wall has to be painted a single hue, and we know from earlier examples that adding color and pattern increases the arousal and curiosity of the viewers. Figure 8.8 provides examples and methods for simple color application techniques to break the visual monotony of interior columns and walls. Experiment with variations of the technique to achieve different color expressions and outcomes.

## COLOR AND THE ELEMENTS

Look for ways you can introduce color variety into your work. Variety is the principle of design that breaks the pattern of rhythmic repetition and can help catch and keep the interest of users of the space. Naturally, people dislike being forced to look at the same object over and over. Variety of shapes, lines, textures, and patterns breaks up the monotony and gives the viewers an array of visual stimuli.

### Color and Line

**Line** is the connection between two points in space. A line can take many forms, including symbolic, as in the lines that create our stars and stripes of the American flag. A line can be used to communicate action, like the arrows in a road sign

**FIGURE 8.7a** The interior of this restaurant space requires key colors to stimulate and introduce the perception of a fine-dining experience. (Illustration by Steven Stankiewicz)

**FIGURE 8.7b** Key design elements are highlighted and contrasted with color, adding variety and visual stimulation in this restaurant space. (Illustration by Steven Stankiewicz)

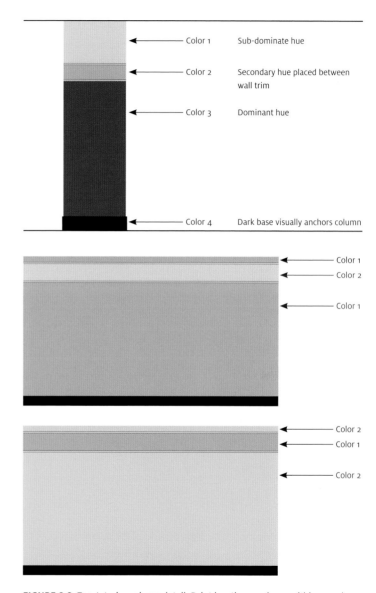

**FIGURE 8.8** Top. Interior column detail. Paint locations on base, within reveal, and upper portion in different values of violet. Middle. Wall elevation illustrating color locations—Option 1. Bottom. Wall elevation illustrating color locations—Option 2.

or the yellow lines that indicate a two-way street. The bark of a tree is a series of jagged lines, which tells us before we touch it that the texture of the bark is rough. Subtle, layered lines of color gracefully indicate the contour of the horizon at sundown. The way in which lines are utilized and combined with color can determine the effectiveness of an interior space. Without line, no other part of a composition could happen. There are four types of lines: vertical, horizontal, diagonal, and curved.

Vertical lines symbolize strength and stability, like the columns that support a building. Verticality provides the upward and downward movement, accentuating height and giving rise to expansive interiors or directing the viewer to the ceiling, where further design details may be present. Use vertical lines to emphasize the height and perception of a larger space. The strength and power of vertical lines are reinforced with strong, warm hues of red, orange, and yellow.

Horizontal lines are restful and remind us of a body at rest. Horizontal lines can break vertical surface planes to decrease the height of space or widen the interior where they are used. Horizontal lines create movement from side to side, reminiscent of the horizon or plateau of a tabletop mountain. Using cool colors with horizontal lines increase the perception and sensation of a space being restful, relaxing, and calm. Horizontal lines lead the eye across an object and emphasize width.

Diagonal lines are dynamic and unusual in that they defy gravity. This line inspires interest and awe while suggesting quick action and radical movement to the viewer. Diagonal lines are effective in informal design planning where a progressive, imaginative solution is required. It tends to give the illusion of instability and uncertainty, and implies potential danger, like a steep slope. This perception can be supported with warm hues such as red, yellow, and orange. Purple, coined a "mysterious" color because it is a combination of polar opposites (red and blue), would also serve well in supporting the impressions conveyed by diagonal lines and angled shapes.

Curved lines are soft, gentle, and fluid. They remind us of femininity, clouds, flowers, and nature. The curved line supported by blues and greens reminds us of nature, water, and growth. Soft pastels, pinks, and red-violets will also make a curved line seem graceful, peaceful, and relaxing. Curvilinear lines are organic and peaceful, and can be combined with sharp right angles and straight lines for contrast and added emphasis. Curved lines are friendly, not abrupt, inviting, and less formal. Frank Gehry, the master of curved lines, uses color and contrast to emphasize the organic shape of the Marqués de Riscal hotel located in Elciego, Spain (Figure 8.9). In this example the red-violet accentuates the curve and adds emphasis to the organic shapes used in the architecture.

## Color and Shape

**Shape** is the result of one or more lines connecting to form a two-dimensional image such as a square, circle, or triangle. Design basics that influence and form the language of all spaces have their roots in the Bauhaus school in Dessau, Germany, started in 1919 by architect Walter Gropius. To identify and provide the viewer with a variety of shapes, textures, and forms reinforced by colors, we can stimulate the senses and create an environment. The circle represents fluid movement, not static, and enables the eye to travel around freely. Variation of circle size and concentric circles can add rhythm and movement to your design. We are naturally drawn to differences—they stand out—and a circle offers a calming softness. Using color for contrast offers more visual variety. The café in the Tate Modern Museum, London, uses vertical lines contrasted against colored circles to add visual drama.

**FIGURE 8.9** Main hotel building of the Marquis De Riscal in Eleciego, Basque County, Spain, designed using pink and gold titanium with stainless steel. Designed by architect Frank Gehry.

(© Colin McPherson/Corbis)

The simple furnishings and dark floor balance the intense pattern and color (Figure 8.10). The selection of color and pattern indicates a modern style and supports the purpose of the museum. A traditional color palette of dark navy and less intense sage green in combination with a traditional **damask** pattern wouldn't be appropriate because it could misrepresent the intended use of the space. The navy blue (shade) and sage green (tone) color palette might work better in a space of quiet contemplation such as a library or study. The loud pattern and color in the café generate excitement and energy, thus encouraging conversation, laughter, and enjoyment of friends and family in a welcoming and playful setting.

The square, a combination of vertical and horizontal lines, is stable and secure with its predictable equal sides; however, when rotated to stand on a corner, it seemingly defies gravity, which could add dynamic variety and a dramatic focal point. The square does not occur organically in nature, and therefore, as a man-made artifice, it calls attention to the artisan's creativity. Strong, saturated colors are supported with this shape. In Figure 8.11, the long corridor of this contemporary office is broken into smaller segments with bands of orange, which in turn shortens the perceived length of the space. Color applied to the soffit and onto the inlaid carpet border creates a square portal that adds rhythm and a transitional experience for visitors.

The rectangle is also a stable shape, adding more variety with two sides varying in width. This shape is more restful than the square when laid on its long axis and just the opposite when positioned on its short axis, where it resembles support columns and strength. A rectangle is a more visually interesting shape than a square, and a rectangular room provides more opportunities for spatial arrangement because it is slightly more complex.

A triangle suggests stability when at rest on its base, and it leads the eye upward toward the sky. Triangles use the dynamic elements of angles and diagonals to create visual movement and energy. The interest of a triangle can be enhanced by applying the color yellow.

The characteristics of shape and color outlined by Itten can be translated into our interior spaces. When color and shape combine, their meanings are intensified, giving the space a soul and a language that speaks to us.

**FIGURE 8.10** Tate Modern Restaurant, London. (© Ludovic Maisant/Hemis/Corbis)

**FIGURE 8.11** Reception desk with translucent panels and orange colored arcades in a contemporary office. (© Tom Sibley/Corbis)

**FIGURE 8.12** (a) Left. Color and pattern create visual texture in this dining space. (b) Right. Removal of the wallcovering eliminates the color contrast and variety. (Left: © Imagemore Co., Ltd./Corbis)

## Color and Texture

**Texture** is the characteristic visual and tactile quality of the surface of a material resulting from the way in which the materials are constructed or combined together. Texture is the aspect of harmony that relates to the sense of touch. This sense may be stimulated either physically or visually. A surface can be smooth or rough like natural stone or a sisal carpet. A colored surface can visually imply texture through the use of striping or bands of color, speckled, or **faux finishes**. Textures can be one of two types: (1) naturally rough, smooth, or **matte** finished materials such as wood, glass, stone, and more, or (2) reflective or translucent surfaces and materials such as high-gloss, semigloss, or **satin** finishes that include glass, acrylics, or paint finishes. The use of materials and finishes add to the variety of a design and well-chosen combinations will provide the sensory and visual contrast needed to make the space more interesting. If all textures are of one type with the exception of one item of a different texture, the distinctive item becomes a point of emphasis or visual interest.

We depend on the tactile sensation of feeling textured surfaces within our environment. This kinetic connection is essential and can be experienced when

colors of different hues and values are combined to create the illusion of texture, when no tactile texture is present. The wall covering in Figure 8.12a is an example of color used to create the appearance of texture. In spaces where there is a limited amount of visual stimulation, separation of activity zones, or the need for contrast of shape, color patterns can be used to add the visual interest needed. The dining space requires visual contrast of pattern, shape, and dark value to add excitement and a backdrop to the dining space. If we remove the wall covering, we lose the variety and visual stimulus the wall covering color and pattern provided to the space (Figure 8.12b).

## Color and Pattern

**Pattern** is the repetitive arrangement of shapes and colors in a systematic horizontal, vertical, diagonal, or organic sequence. Color pattern and texture applications are the easiest and quickest methods for adding variety into your projects.

Neutral color harmonies.

Complementary color harmonies.

Analogous color harmonies.

**FIGURE 8.13** Color, pattern, and texture add variety to color harmonies.

**FIGURE 8.14** Opposite page. Brightly colored interior of Miami Airport, with light falling through colorful Perspex strips, creating multicolored patterns on the floor. (© Barry Lewis/Corbis)

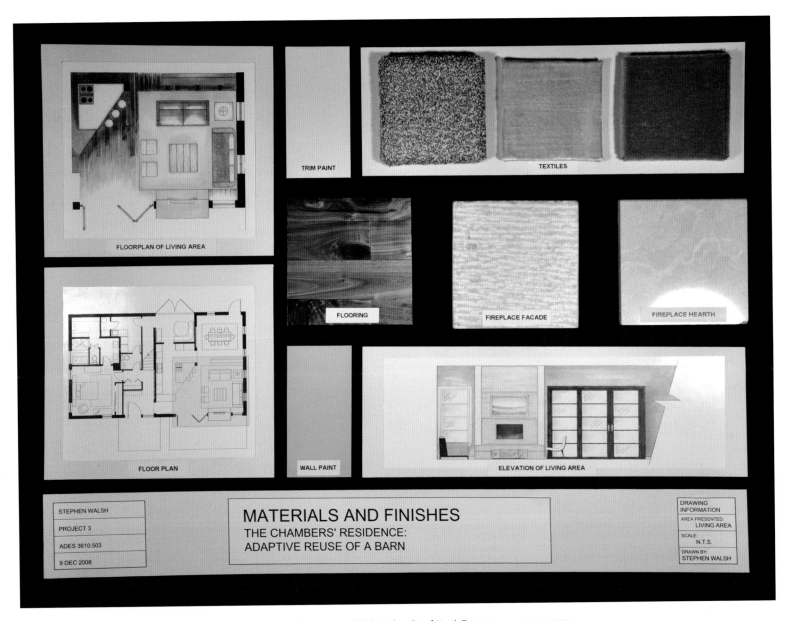

**FIGURE 8.15** Example of a color plan for a residential space by student Stephen Walsh, University of North Texas. (Courtesy, Stephen Walsh)

The key, again, is to limit the variety; otherwise, the pieces may not fit to make a whole. Figure 8.13 illustrates the use of color, pattern, and texture to create variety within a series of color palettes. Color patterns can be the result of transmitted light through transparent material such as glass or plastic. The colored glass panels in Figure 8.14 create a kaleidoscope of colorful striped patterns on the floor of the Miami Airport. The use of colored glass is an effective way of designing with intense colors; however, the transparency filters light and allows the color to be enjoyed without the intense saturation of pigment paint that could create visual overstimulation.

There is an enormous variety of wood types, plastic laminates, marbles, stone, tiles, textiles, metals, colored glass, and more available for design projects. Technological advances have made production processes more versatile, offering an endless array of material to use in your design work. If it isn't stressful enough that paint is offered in thousands of colors, add that to the thousands of materials on the market, and the color combination and varieties of visual experiences are limitless. Creating a color plan is an important part of communicating your design intention to a client (Figure 8.15). Careful attention needs to be paid to all of the principles of design we have discussed and how color can combine with these to accentuate the built environment.

Variety is a powerful element for adding interest, contrasts, and life within an interior space. Using color in your projects should be an enjoyable and meaningful experience for both you and your clients. With each new project, you'll continue to learn about color complexities and the ways in which you can use color to give your work personality. Use of color with intention and informed research will ensure a successful color solution.

To experience design is to experience the world and the personal connections that occur in our built environment. Our experiences shape our spaces, and our spaces, in turn, shape us. Color, masterfully coordinated with the principles of balance, rhythm, emphasis, proportion, scale, unity, harmony, and variety, is the designer's most expressive tool.

## KEY WORDS
Variety, contrast, line, shape, damask, texture, faux finishes, matte, satin, pattern

## LEARNING OUTCOMES
- Use the right amount of variety in colors to create or modify an interior.
- Rooms that are too simple or "boxlike" can become more visually interesting if one or more elements in the space are treated with color to differentiate those elements from the other design features in the room.
- Avoid impulsive uses of color—this can provide too much variety that lacks unity and harmony within the space.
- Colored light and colored translucent materials can add to the visual variety; however, be constantly aware of the amount and type of light source (natural or artificial) that is to be used, and control it. Excessive light can add to much visual contrast and upset the color varieties intended.
- Using color with line, shape, texture, and pattern gives the designer the capacity to add visual stimuli and create a variety of experiences for users of the built environment.

## EXERCISES
1. Is texture, pattern, or contrast more predominant in a color scheme? Select a series of interior images, and discuss how each of the elements affects the variety of colored spaces.
2. If there is no pattern in a room, how can texture, contrast, and color intensities create variety? Discuss and give visual examples, from your own portfolio or from magazines and Web sites, to explain the idea.
3. Take a common natural object, and model the object abstractly using color, pattern, and texture. Use the character of the original object to influence the model prototype now redefined into a usable object (e.g., a light fixture, piece of furniture, storage element, or structural feature).

color + culture

9

In the United States, color symbolism abounds: red for stop or "red-blooded," green for go or "green with envy," yellow for caution or "yellow-bellied coward," white for purity and virginity, blue for water and the skies above or for that sad day when you just want to be "singing the blues," brown for the richness of soil, and so on (Morton, 1997, pp. 40–41).

Appreciation and respect for cultural differences is important during the color design process. We cannot assume that for every client our own color meanings and symbolism reach across individual and cultural differences. The influences of Asia, Latin America, and the Middle East require us to understand differing interpretations of color among diverse cultures, and in doing so, we enrich our own lives and the lives of people we design for.

Many design firms are crossing oceans and contracting work with other nations, setting up satellite offices, and embarking in design that embraces cultural differences. Up to this point in the book, we have examined the processes of using color in the interior space. It is easy to view color through a narrow lens, never once considering that color meaning and cultural traditions influence color, and therefore differences among individuals will vary and depart from those of Western traditions or our own personal associations. A cultural sensitivity should be taken into consideration during the planning of design projects, especially in public spaces where there are opportunities for various cultures to experience these spaces.

A bride in America is expected to dress in white as a symbol of purity, whereas this color represents death and mourning in several Asian cultures. Many factors, including geography, religion, tradition, and shifting political power, can contribute to a wide cultural difference in color meaning, preference, and symbolism. No one source is the authority on color diversity because it changes as each new generation embarks on making its own mark in the historical timeline. Wars, revolutions, disasters, and change in leadership can bring about a new era of color meanings. Whatever the future may hold, understanding the past is critical to understanding the future.

"Lifestyle is intimately connected with taste in colors . . . however; some widely used basic colors can fit into any type of lifestyle" (Kobayashi, 1990, p. 17).

Kobayashi identifies eight lifestyles/tastes that most people fit into: casual, modern, romantic, natural, elegant, chic, classic, and dandy or masculine (pp. 18–19). Variations exist among sources, and generalizations have been drawn to indicate the common color meanings among the cultures explored in this chapter. An infinite number of color meanings are possible, and aside from surveying the population of these nations, no book of this size would scratch the surface of the many nations to be explored. Just as color is vast, so are the preferences and perceptions of people among each nation. Whether influenced by fashion trends or politics, a study of color meanings can shed light on the ideological differences that exist in this world.

It is important to note that I have chosen to focus primarily on the positive associations, with the exceptions of those colors that represent death and mourning. I encourage you in your color research to seek the duality of meanings to avoid design solutions that may impart negative reactions or memories of tragic events to certain individuals. For our purposes, we will examine five nations in the regions of Latin America (Mexico), Europe (Italy), North Africa (Morocco), Central Asia (Pakistan), and Eastern Asia (Japan). With so many wonderful countries and cultures to highlight, I've included those that represent a cross section of our globe. It is my hope that you will be inspired by the cultures presented to research others in your color studies.

## MEXICO

When you think of Latin America, a culture of vivid, bright, saturated colors comes to mind. A spectrum of color is common in Mexican architecture and interiors (Figure 9.1). Mexican color in architecture and design draws upon its Aztec heritage. Temples of ancient Mayan and Aztec cities used color to represent cardinal directions. Rooms facing east were decorated in gold, west in turquoise blue, south in white, and north in red. Spanish influence in Mexico brought about the use of natural materials to create colored dyes in rich reds, blues, and yellow. These included cochineal, indigo, and sea snails. Dark blue to purple is commonly worn to symbolize mourning and death. Cemeteries in Mexico use vibrant colors to celebrate the passing on of their kin. Mexican textiles and decorative

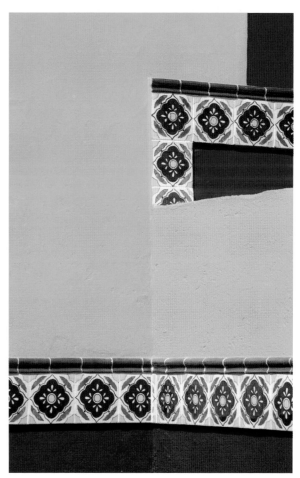

FIGURE 9.1 Left. Explosion of Latin colors in San Jose, Costa Rica. Bottom. Rich, vivid hues in Cabo San Lucas architecture. (Left: © Ron Niebrugge/Alamy; bottom: © Daniel J. Cox/Corbis)

FIGURE 9.2 Above. Colorful wall with hand-made tile work, Guanajuato, Mexico. (© Julie Eggers/Corbis)

tiles are further examples of the prolific use of vibrant colors (Figure 9.2). Typical Mexican clothing consists of a rainbow of hues of yellow, green, aqua, red, and white. Colorful blankets based on Mayan textiles are key decorative elements in Mexican homes. Red and blue colors are used in attracting the gods, with blue relating to the heavens, sky, and tranquility.

The conquest of the Aztecs by the Spaniards brought about a cultural shift where indigenous people were demoted to a lower class and not permitted to have or use gold. Gold was used extensively in cathedrals and other public buildings. The poor began to use tin as a replacement for gold, and it continues to be a predominant material in Mexican arts and design.

**FIGURE 9.3** Top. Mexico's national flag waves in the foreground of Mexico City. (© Reuters/Corbis)

**FIGURE 9.4** Bottom. Example of a Spanish colonial interior. (© Michael Freeman/Corbis)

**FIGURE 9.5** A hand-carved wooden bed and built-in storage are shrouded in bold blue and gold hues adorning this bedroom in San Miguel de Allende, Mexico. (© Craig Lovell/Eagle Visions Photography/Alamy)

**FIGURE 9.6** Top. Lobby of the Paraiso de la Bonita resort and spa located along the Mexican Caribbean. Right. Interior of a seventeenth-century building in Oaxaca, located in southern Mexico. Bottom. A resort bedroom at Casa Tigre del Mar, Costa Careyes, Mexico. (Top: © Ludovic Maisant/Corbis; right: © Robert Fried/Alamy; bottom: © Massimo Listri/Corbis)

The Mexican flag (Figure 9.3) consists of green, white, and red, with the center coat of arms symbolizing Aztec heritage. Green signifies hope, white stands for unity, and red stands for heroes who shed blood in the efforts for independence (Xerox, 2008, p. 1). The interior in Figure 9.4 is predominately white, common in **Spanish colonial** interiors, with accents of red in the tapestries, rugs, and textiles representative of the national flag. The Spanish colonial style consisted of hand-carved wood furnishings, heavy wooden ceiling beams, stucco walls, and **Saltillo** tiled floors, as shown in the interior.

Bright blue is frequently used in Mexican homes to defend against evil spirits. Yellow represent the sun and fire (Figure 9.5), with blue symbolizing wisdom, peace, truth, and the heavens above and sea below. Rich terra-cotta red and burnt sienna taken from the pigment and soil of the landscape are commonplace for Mexican interiors (Figure 9.6). The work of architect Luis Barragan has brought a modernist sensibility to the ancient Aztec architects while using the bright, bold

**color + culture**

**FIGURE 9.7** Left. Mexican Talavera pottery in bright, bold colors. Bottom. Pillars of Church of San Francisco Acatepec, Cholula, Mexico.

(Left: © Massimo Listri/Corbis; bottom: © Radius Images/Alamy)

hues of contemporary Mexican culture to weave the thread of history and emotion associated with Mexico's past. The landscape of Mexico influences the palette used in their architecture, design, and arts. Tropical plants, cacti, the alamanda flower with its hues of pink, peach, and yellow, bougainvillea, and sunflowers have all been sources of color and meaning for the Mexican people. Places of worship are often highly decorated in tiles of many colors and patterns. The Church of San Francisco of Acatepec is an example of the Baroque influence in Mexico. The façade and interior are adorned in blue, black, orange, green, yellow, and brown Talavera tiles. Talavera is a Mexican pottery that originated in the region of Talavera in the province of Toledo, Spain (Figure 9.7).

At the center of Mexican culture is the *Dia de los Muertos*, or **Day of the Dead**. This celebration, held yearly in October, honors those who have passed. Skeletons and colors of orange and pink are common among this celebration that represents the return of lost souls. Figure 9.8 illustrates modern shopping malls in Cabo San Lucas and Ixtapa, Mexico, using the traditional purples, green, orange, and pink. Xochimilco canals south of Mexico City are a popular attraction, where brightly colored trajineras (gondolas) are used for holidays and tourists (Figure 9.9).

Even as the landscape of Mexico becomes modernized, the traditional bright hues continue to reflect the cultural heritage evident in residential neighborhoods. The bright colors common in Aztec and Mexican culture is taken directly from their landscape, the skyline, and vivid green plant life. The *fiesta* is celebrated and recognized with the use of bright reds and yellows. The Mexican landscape reflects colonial, coastal, and modern approaches to living, but at the heart lies color, the essence of life for Mexican people, and a way to remember their past and celebrate their future.

## ITALY

The epicenter of some of the most beautiful examples of Renaissance architecture and design, Italy's rich landscape and cobblestoned streets and canals offer the eye a kaleidoscope of colors. The work of Leonardo da Vinci, Raphael, and Michelan-

**FIGURE 9.8**  Left. Colorful Mexican shopping mall, Ixtapa, Mexico. (© Chuck Keeler, Jr./Corbis)

**FIGURE 9.9**  Bottom. Colorful *trajineras* (gondolas), Mexico City, Mexico. (© Digital Vision/Alamy)

gelo add to the rich culture and decadent lifestyle supported by strong, vibrant colors of Italy. The color sienna, a reddish brown hue, derived its name from the city of Sienna in Italy where stucco façades are painted in this hue. The city of Magenta in the province of Milan is another example of color naming often associated with the color heritage of a particular culture. Naples yellow is a lead-based paint used in ceramics and painting as early as the 1500s. The pigment was an originally made in Naples, Italy, where the natural pigment of the color was taken from the earth near Mount Vesuvius. Lead is no longer used in the manufacturing of Naples yellow due to its harmful effects. The color is commonly seen in Tuscan palettes alongside terra-cotta (brownish red) in tile flooring and wall mosaics, and leafy greens reminiscent of the Italian countryside (Figure 9.10).

The Italian flag, composed of green for hope, white for faith, and red for charity, was adopted in 1796 and became the symbol of freedom and unity (Figure 9.11). The Italian government has gone so far as to adopt descriptive terms for its flag in an attempt to express and reflect the culture of Italy: "meadow green, milk white, and tomato red" (http://www.flagspot.net). Red and green symbolize the Catholic faith in Italy, along with gold for divinity, as seen in the beautiful churches of Rome. Red is worn for good luck in the New Year, and surprisingly, the giving of red underwear is common (Morton, 2004, p. 56). Green symbolizes the landscape of spring and youthfulness. Blue represents the heavens, and purple—a combination of blue and red—represents death and mourning. In addition to black being used to mark the death of a loved one, the death of young child is mourned by the wearing of white.

Italian homes are splendidly decorated, showing an effort to express their individuality with red tiled roofs, brightly painted walls, and a lush palette of colors from foods, the landscape, and the sea that surrounds Italy. Brightly colored pottery adorns many homes in Italy (Figure 9.12). Decorative ceramic tiles are an important material used in the design of Italian homes. These tiles are highly detailed with arabesques, floras, herbs, and geometric patterns in hues of the Italian landscape (Figure 9.13). The traditional home reflects a stronger direct

**FIGURE 9.10** Italian kitchen interior colored in Naples yellow. (© 2006 LOOK Photography)

**FIGURE 9.11** Above. Italian national flag. (© Caro /Alamy)

**FIGURE 9.12** Right. An assortment of ceramics reflecting the diverse tradition of pottery in Italy. (Red Cover)

**FIGURE 9.13** Opposite page. Italian tile work adorning the wall of this foyer. (© Massimo Listri/Corbis)

use of color and pattern, whereas the modern Italian home represents a contemporary lifestyle among ancient Roman ruins. The love of history and design, both traditional and modern, has led to many interior interpretations of the colors, styling, and details of Italian interiors (Figure 9.14).

The beauty of Italy is unquestionable. Past and present intertwine in an explosion of vibrant hues with a rich heritage, fine furnishings, fashion, and personal style of the Italian culture.

## PAKISTAN

Pakistan is a relatively young country, having gained its independence from India in 1947. The country's primary religion is Islam, and it is one of the largest Muslim states in the world. Vivid color is an important part of Pakistan culture commonly expressed in green, white, gold, red, and black. Emerald green is the color of the national flag and is the most popular color symbolizing life and Islam (Figure 9.15). The flag of Pakistan marks its independence with a green and white

**FIGURE 9.14** Top. Traditional Italian interior. Right. Modern Italian interior. Notice the continued use of rich red hues alongside natural wood finishes. (Top: © BUILT Images/ Alamy; right: © Cristina Fumi/Alamy)

field with the emblem of a five-point star and crescent. The crescent symbolizes progress, and the star represents light and knowledge. The larger field of green represents the majority Muslim population, and the white stripe the minority populations. The color green is evident in their culture and can be seen in the team colors for their national game of cricket (Figure 9.16).

Green and white are evident in Pakistan's architecture, most notably in its mosque tilework. Green is associated with the Islamic religion, nature, and life. Figure 9.17 illustrates a nineteenth-century mosaic of ceramic fragments predominantly in green and white. Marriage is a highly celebrated festival in Pakistan. Prior to the wedding, two events are hosted: **Mayoun** (celebration of the bride) and **Mehendi** (celebration of the groom). Yellow is the color worn by a bride in a simple **shalwar kameez** or loose pajama-like clothing to be worn during Mayoun. During Mehendi, an event hosted by the groom's family, shades of green and yellow are worn. It is during this ceremony the bride's hands and feet are decorated with henna. Red is strongly associated with women in Pakistan and is traditionally worn during wedding ceremonies (Figure 9.18), while the traditional white **sherwani**, a long coatlike coat garment embroidered in gold, is worn by men. It is customary for the bride to receive a package of garments from the groom's family, neatly wrapped and displayed a week before the wedding day. This package is called a **bari**. Women also wear bangles as a sign of marriage in contrast to the wedding ring in America. They come in a variety of red, green, and yellow colors.

The national flower of Pakistan is the white jasmine, used in weddings, celebrations, and religious events and worn on Friday, a holiday. Blue is regarded as a protective color, and in periods of mourning, women wear black and men wear white. Purple is generally disliked by Pakistani men. Black represents divine truth or beauty and is commonly worn by Muslim women. Getting to know the character, history, traditions, and customs of a particular culture will bring sensibility to your design work. Selecting color for projects goes beyond the aesthetics and fashionable trends. Understanding the traditions and social graces of your clients will prepare you to make accurate and pleasing color choices.

**FIGURE 9.15** Pakistan's national flag. (© JUPITERIMAGES/Comstock Images/Alamy)

**FIGURE 9.16** The color green repeats in Pakistan's team colors. (© Andy Clark/Reuters/Corbis)

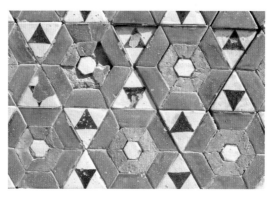

**FIGURE 9.17** A Pakisani mosaic tile pattern of triangles and hexagons in green, white, and blue, subtly representing the star of the national flag. (© Christine Osborne/Corbis)

The Basant Festival of kites welcomes spring into Pakistan. A myriad of spring colors, yellow predominantly, is worn to celebrate the seasonal change. The Baluch people of western Pakistan are known for their highly ornate and detailed textile work. These textiles are often dyed with a spectrum of colorful, bright hues, embellished with floral and geometric patterns. The **kalamandi**, or "inkpot," images common in Baluch rugs are large hexagons filled with stylized patterns including trees (Figure 9.19).

## MOROCCO

Situated in the northwest region of Africa, Morocco is a country of diverse cultural influences. With close proximity to Spain, Portugal, and France, these countries have done much to influence the Moroccan culture, which is considered the gateway to the Arab world. Moroccan carpets, carvings, ceramics, and weavings are common designed objects used in homes. The elaborate Mediterranean styling

**FIGURE 9.18** Pakistani brides wear the traditional ceremonial color red in a collective wedding in Multan, Pakistan. (© MK Chaudry/epa/Corbis)

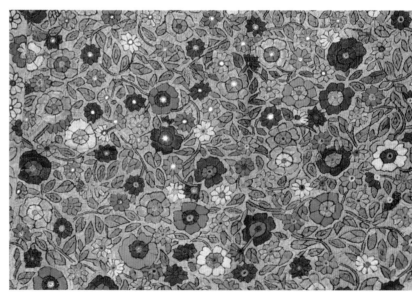

**FIGURE 9.19** Left. Pakistani hand-woven and vegetable-died Baluch rugs. Above. Baluch textile work from Pakistan in rich, vibrant hues. (Left: Veer; above: © Christine Osborne/Corbis)

**FIGURE 9.20** Moroccan national flag.

(© David Sutherland/Corbis)

**FIGURE 9.21** Top. Traditional blue-painted doors. (© David Sutherland/Corbis)

**FIGURE 9.22** Bottom. Colorful Mediterranean coastline. (© 2006 Hemera Technologies/JupiterImages)

is largely sought after for home décor in the west and seen extensively in U.S. retailers. Color in Moroccan design is bold, with bright blues, yellows, and muted oranges. Colors of natural foods are often sources for design inspiration, including eggplant, olives, and saffron spice. Like many countries, the flag is a national symbol of pride where one can find color meanings for a particular culture. The Moroccan flag of red symbolizes the prophet Mohammed, and the green star symbolizes life, wisdom, and good health, in addition to the Islamic religion (Figure 9.20). Green and red are among the favorite colors of its people.

Walking through the streets of Morocco, a curious Western eye will ponder at the plethora of blue-painted doors, windows, and shutters. A tradition dating back to early Egyptian times, blue is used to ward off evil and to protect from the "evil eye." Light blue is commonly painted on the front of Moroccan doors and window shutters (Figure 9.21). Red, royal blues, emerald greens, brilliant gold, and purple symbolize royalty and riches in Morocco. White is commonly worn on Fridays and special occasions and is frequently painted on the exterior of homes. The white illuminates the interior by reflecting the natural light surrounding the window and window sill into the home and in turn deflecting unwanted heat, keeping the interior cool. Interiors are a kaleidoscope of colors using aquamarine and turquoise to reflect the beauty of the cool, aquatic Mediterranean coastline (Figure 9.22).

Beautifully designed carpets and tiles are common in Moroccan interiors. The Berbers, first inhabitants of Northern Africa, created elaborate handspun carpets and rugs. The name is synonymous with the style—reflecting the colors of the landscape and natural materials that were used to make the colored dyes of beige, brown, saffron, terra-cotta, and cinnamon (Figure 9.23). These carpets were mainly used for bedding and blankets of the nomadic Berber tribe. The carpet pile ranged from long and thick for colder climates to short and dense for warmer climates. Today, Berber carpets are known for their durability and speckled appearance, reflecting the natural characteristics of the original Berber tradition.

The rich blend of culture and tradition defines the exotic color palettes of Moroccan culture. Whether terra-cotta ceramics, aquamarine and turquoise textured walls, or the brilliant blues, purples, and crimsons of the tile work, the culture of Morocco is a sweet treat of color for the beholder. Moroccan interiors consist of thousands of tiny tiles arranged in complex mosaics in a variety of vibrant hues (Figure 9.24). Moroccan tiles can be seen covering every interior surface from floor, to wall, to ceiling.

## JAPAN

Japan is a small island with approximately 127 million people. Religion plays a significant part in Japanese culture, with 94 percent practicing Buddhism. The Buddhist faith influences all aspects of Japanese life, evident in its architecture, art, and literature. Buddhist homes often have small altars ornately decorated with photographs of deceased family members. Dragons are a common symbol in Japan and represent power, strength, and wisdom. Often portrayed in vibrant hues of pink and violet, they are present during celebrations and adorn many gardens as water fountains. The ceiling of the Japanese temple in Figure 9.25 is elaborately adorned with gold dragons.

Color in Japan can vary between bright and gaudy to muted and natural. The interiors of Japanese homes are modest, refined, and elegant. Rooms serve multiple purposes as a family room, dining room, and bedroom. Traditional opaque sliding **fusuma** doors, or shoji panels, made of wood and paper, can screen for privacy to create a bedroom (Figure 9.26). These doors can be opened to create larger spaces or closed for intimate occasions. Geometry and proportioning of interior space is essential to the Japanese desire for order and the Eastern philosophy of simplicity.

Brighter garish colors of red, yellow, blue, orange, and green are often reserved for shrines and sacred places of worship. In the home, the family shrine is commonly adorned in ebony black, gold, and deep reds (Figure 9.27). Orange, commonly seen in dishware and textiles, represents the knowledge and civilization of Japan. Colors are found in many building materials in Japanese homes, including stone, paper, bamboo, cane, and cedar and maple woods. When color is introduced into the home, it is usually in the form of a single hue used as a strong point of interest. Figure 9.28 shows a traditional Japanese living room with the far wall painted in a shade of olive green, reinforcing the connection with nature. There is a balance of space, form, textures, and natural materials in Japanese culture. The interior colors are an extension of the Japanese landscape used in the home interior to bring harmony between life and nature.

Wedding white in Western society symbolizes purity; in Japan, the women will wear the classical white kimono for purity, but more to symbolize their

**FIGURE 9.25** Left. Dragon motif in a Japanese temple. (© Michael Hitoshi/Taxi/Getty Images)

**FIGURE 9.26** Bottom. Japanese fusuma doors open this space and connects nature to the interior. (© Danita Delimont/Alamy)

departure or death from their family (Figure 9.29). The Japanese flag is white with a red circle that symbolizes the sun (Figure 9.30). The combination of red and white on the flag is commonly used in the wedding ceremony and frequents dining spaces as a strong hue combined with black lacquers (Figure 9.31). Purple represents royalty and nobility, a ceremonial color, and is prohibited in weddings. Blue symbolizes youthfulness—unlike in North America, where green has this association. During times of war among dynasties, warriors were known to

**FIGURE 9.27** Left. Family shrine, Sapporo, Hokkaido, Japan. (© Michael Freeman/Corbis)

**FIGURE 9.28** Bottom left. Japanese living room that uses natural colors and materials to form a simplistic interior. It also provides a sense of peace with its geometric order. (© Photodisc/Alamy)

**FIGURE 9.29** Bottom middle. Japanese bride on her wedding day in a classical white kimono at the Meiji Shrine. (© Andrew Holbrooke/Corbis)

**FIGURE 9.30** Bottom right. Japanese national flag. (© Wolfgang Deuter/zefa/Corbis)

**FIGURE 9.31** Japanese-style dining room, with a traditional and elegant red hue. (© Photodisc/Alamy)

wear a yellow chrysanthemum as a symbol of courage in battle. The yellow chry-santhemum used in Japanese gardens may be the only color and/or flower used. The chrysanthemum flower is commonly displayed in Japanese porcelain along with other bold colors. While colors are ever present in the Japanese culture, the hues and textures of their native landscape provided balance and emotional harmony. Silver and gray are commonly used to represent maturity and old age. Japan is a land of rich history and balanced lifestyle.

As the divide among cultures shrinks, designers will be required to consider the cultural differences among clients when preparing color solutions for proj-ects. Your success can be increased through careful color planning that engages you in researching these differences. You will benefit and appreciate the rich, colorful diversity on our planet. To expand upon the cultures presented so far, a quick overview of color meanings and symbolism for China, Korea, Ireland, and Egypt is shown in Table 9.1.

**TABLE 9.1** Cross-Cultural Color Symbolism (China, Korea, Ireland, and Egypt)

| HUE | CHINA | KOREA | IRELAND | EGYPT |
|---|---|---|---|---|
| RED | Good luck, happiness, and celebration | "Power and authority, high class and luxury"; some Koreans believe the color can prevent "misfortune," and as such, it is the color for the Korean soccer team | Red wool is believed to relieve sore throats | Death, historically, Egyptians associated themselves as "red people" and used natural materials to dye their skin red |
| BLUE | Represents the heavens, clouds, and immortality | Darker values associated with death | Peace and truth | Virtue, faith, wards off evil |
| GREEN | Infidelity of women when worn in clothing; youthfulness | Life, youth, prosperity | Represent Catholicism (national flag), shamrock for luck | National color, commonly used on mosque and places of worship, symbolizes fertility and strength |
| YELLOW | Wealth, power, imperial color of the Qing dynasty, masculine | "Relates to the sun, energy and rich harvesting of the fall" | Favorite color among people | Prosperity, mourning, eternity |
| PURPLE | Not popular among residents | Wealth, inner peace | Rosaries of the Catholic faith are commonly amethyst and represents cardinal direction east | Favored color of Cleopatra, used Purpura snails for dye, faith |
| ORANGE | Happiness and good health | Result of yellow (energy) and red (power and love), orange represents cheerfulness and often is associated with youth because of its "casual" nature | Represents Protestants (national flag) because of William of Orange, the Protestant English king | Not used in ancient times; however, iron oxides and coppers were used with other minerals to produce red and green paints |
| BLACK | Water | Color of trigrams in their national flag, representing the elements of fire, water, earth, wood, and metal | Represents the devil and cardinal direction north | Dignity, luck, rebirth |
| WHITE | Death and mourning | Innocence, purity | Unity of two faiths (Catholic and Protestant) and represents cardinal direction south | Sacred, holy, used in ceremonial activities, joy |

Contributions for Korea: Jin Gyu, Phillip Park of University of North Texas

In closing, color and design shape behavior, behavior shapes culture, and culture shapes design. Our world is ever changing, and design is ever evolving. "What is true of the chair is true of all the artifacts we create . . . we design them; but once built, they shape us" (Cranz, 1998, p. 15).

## KEY WORDS
Spanish colonial, Saltillo, Day of the Dead, Mayoun, Mehendi, shalwar kameez, sherwani, bari, kalamandi, fusuma

## LEARNING OUTCOMES
- Develop knowledge of the historical, cultural, and symbolic meanings of color.
- Religious, political, and social values shape color symbolism and meaning.
- A nation's flag is an excellent inroad to exploring regional differences in color symbolism.
- Color planning should consider cross-cultural differences.

## EXERCISES
1. You are taking on the role of a designer or design team preparing conceptual ideas and imagery for a presentation to a local museum for an upcoming exhibit on Culture, Color, and Design. Select a country or culture of your choice, and prepare a conceptual board (11 by 17 or 18 by 24) to include textiles, magazine clippings of interiors, objects, symbols, and decorative items (textiles, pottery, art, sculpture) that reflect the selected country's culture and use of color.

2. Prepare a brief two- to three-page page report of differences in color meanings between two cultures/countries. This project can be done individually or in a group. Select from the following cultures: African, Native American, Indian, German, Russian, Romanian, Swedish, Thai, Australian, Hawaiian, Guatemalan, Indonesian, Jamaican, and Dutch.

3. Historical color palettes represent preferences for color schemes that were predominately used by certain cultures or individuals or that were popular during a specific time period. These palettes are often representative of the social climate during their time of development and offer a window into the design of a historical period. Historical color harmonies can provide a relief from the market saturation of color trends. Many paint manufacturers recognize this and have developed color palettes based on period color harmonies. Studying authentic historical examples of color harmonies will expand your skills in creating as well as recognizing classic combinations that have stood the test of time. How would you design a room if you were commissioned to represent a decade of the past? Choose a decade and create a concept board.

4. Research the history of your ancestors, and create a collage that represents the color and heritage of your background. Provide a brief written statement of your research findings to support your collage design.

# afterword

Like all designers, we learn the hard-and-fast rules in practice. The world is a far different place than the classroom, and you have to be ready at any given moment to quickly adjust, find fast solutions, and work effectively to communicate with your clients. Many of my own color errors occurred in practice, through which I have learned to avoid many of the color design problems that were never presented in academia. Color is a little science, a little art, and a little intuition. Color is always at the top of the list when you are working in design, and it should be considered in the very early stages of the design process.

Color can't be avoided, so it is unnecessary to fit it into any one category and break it down to point that we lose the mere fact that it is a sensation—an emotional experience—that necessitates an open mind and freedom to explore within boundaries. Fear is the primary emotion I see from clients when we work with color. Clients have made a decision, and there is a risk that they will hate the color that is placed in their space, not realizing that it is fluid, changeable, and, with paint, the least expensive item to work with. The furnishings and materials, in my professional opinion, should come after the main color palette selections have been made and the client is at ease with those choices. In that regard, the other more expensive items can be selected with less anxiety, and the project will be a great success.

With any project, the goal is to achieve precise and planned results from deliberate and masterful color usage. Working with paint chips or small colored samples is fine in the initial selection process, but these are far from reliable when magnified a thousand times in a space. Narrow your selections with a client to the top two or three options, then purchase rather inexpensive sample jars that are now available on the market in hundreds of colors, or at the very least, purchase a quart of paint. Use a sheet of white foam-core board (24 by 36 or 20 by 30,

depending on the size available at your local art supply store). Using a sponge artist brush, paint the surface of the foam board in each of the color options. Tack the corners down to prevent bowing, and let it dry.

This tool can now be pinned on wall surfaces in various locations of the space to examine under different lighting conditions and in relation to other materials and colors in the room. This same concept can be used for woods, carpets, and fabrics. The key is this: Do not work with small samples when making color decisions.

## SOCIALLY RESPONSIBLE USE OF COLOR

Interior designers, more than ever, are encouraged to consider the environmental impact of our interior design projects. Ecological consciousness should by now be commonplace and therefore evident in our work.

I leave you with a task. Color comes in a variety of materials (paints, metals, wood, plastics, glass, and paper samples), to name a few. As consumer of products and designers who specify, I encourage you with each project to consider the long-term effects of the use of color media on the environment. Your eco-challenge is to research and use products that are socially responsible. Paint manufactures such as Sherwin-Williams and Benjamin offer color products that are low in volatile organic compounds (VOCs) that have minimum impact on the air quality of the interior space. Materials that are recycled or made from post-consumer materials help alleviate detrimental impacts on the environment.

Visit the Web site for the United States Green Building Council (http://www.usgbc.org) for more information on retailers and strategies to make your projects GREEN!

# color theory history

The following historical timeline adapted from Connie B. D'Imperio, http://www.coloryourcarpet.com, tracks the chronological evolution of the use of colored mattered using colorants and dyes.

**1611** Finland—The oldest known color system is credited to astronomer, priest, and Neo-Platonist Aron Sigfrid Forsius (1569–1637). In his color circle , between the colors black and white, red has been placed on the one side since the classical antiquity, and blue on the other; yellow then comes between white and red, pale yellow between white and yellow, orange between yellow and red.

**1613** Belgium—Franciscus Aguilonius (1567–1617) was a Jesuit priest in Brussels when his color diagram appeared in 1613 in a work on optics. It is possibly the oldest system to use the trio of red, yellow, and blue wherein colors are defined within a linear division.

**1656** Carman, a transparent magenta lake, replaced dragon's blood and madder lake; none were really permanent.

**1659** Holland—Rembrandt (c.1606–1669) Dutchman artist Rembrandt understood the color theory that yellow darkened to brown and red was half yellow, so it too darkened to brown. A problem arises when the brown is darkened with black instead of its opposite color, ultramarine blue.

**1672** England—Isaac Newton (1642–1726) devises the first color wheel. His theory "Optics" had the right idea, dividing the prism and bringing it back together again. However, he chooses the wrong colors—magenta and cyan were missing. Magenta doesn't show up in a crystal spectrum. It was 32 years later before his color theory was published.

**1700** English vermilion dark is developed, a synthetic similar to the cool dark Chinese vermilion, antimony vermilion, mercuric sulfide vermilion (which will blacken some colors), mercuric iodide vermilion (impermanent), and eosine vermilion (with the fugitive coal-tar dye eosine). Since all are opaque today, cadmium red is a better choice and cheaper. The color is almost the same.

**1705** Bister is developed, a transparent yellow-to-brown, duel-tone color made from charred beech wood. It's mainly a water-color pigment.

**1724** Prussian blue is developed, a dual-tone transparent color that was getting close to cyan in its transparent undertone. The deep mass color has a black-green quality that produces a "dirty purple"—but nice greens. Heated Prussian blue made a permanent Prussian brown.

**1731** France—Jacques Christopher Le Blon (1667–1742) invents the fundamental three-color palette and demonstrates his system with many dyes; however, he did not extend his ideas to a properly organized color system.

**1755** Germany—Mathematician Johann Tobias Mayer (1723–1762) develops color theory by math, and his selection of triad colors (red, blue, and yellow) created the hexahedric color solid. Two years later, Mayer tried to identify the exact number of colors that the eye is capable of perceiving.

**1766** England—The first known use of a color wheel is developed by Moses Harris (1731–1785). This one had red, yellow, and blue, but he included black as the only neutral.

**1772** Germany—Astronomer J. Heinrich Lambert (1728–1777) presents the first three-dimensional color system.

**1772** Austria—Ignaz Schiffermüller publishes his color circle in Vienna based on four colors: red, blue, green, and yellow.

**1775** Germany—Tobias Mayer's color triangle is first published by the Göttinger physicist George Christopher Lichtenberg.

**1780** Cobalt blue imitation is developed. Cobalt aluminate blue spinel replaced natural cobalt calcined oxide by 1802, synthetic cobalt never produces the original color again.

**1788** Emerald green is developed, a copper arsenate (and the most poisonous color) that can't be matched by any other element. Also, it turns lead and cadmium to black.

**1788** England—Mosas Harris and Gainsborough make an 18-color wheel, again with no cyan or magenta. They also place ultramarine blue opposite orange, a long-lived mistake.

**1790** England—A new color wheel is developed, the first made for light instead of pigments. Uses red, green, and blue as primaries and is credited to Movwell of Great Britain.

**1809** Germany—Philipp Otto Runge's color wheel has white at the top and black on bottom. Also, the colors wrap around the middle of the sphere, and he chooses the wrong primary colors: red, yellow, and blue opaque plus the pigment black for shades.

**1800** Artists have a transparent triad palette in tubes for the first time. The three mixed into a neutral dark that could be pushed warm or cool.
1. Transparent duel-toned indian yellow.
2. Transparent duel-toned madder lake (close to magenta).
3. Prussian blue, an iron-based transparent color close to cyan.

**1810** Germany—Johann Wolfgang von Goethe (1749–1832) makes a double intersecting triangle color wheel—a six-color wheel without magenta or cyan. Blood red was opposite emerald green, instead of cyan.

**1810** Germany—The painter Philipp Otto Runge introduces his version of a color-sphere construction after eight years of work with colors.

**1826** Permanent alizarin is discovered in natural root madder lake. The purpurin was subtracted with sulfuric acid.

**1828** Synthetic ultramarine blue is developed, made from clay, soda, sulfur, coal, and heat.

**1839** France—A twelve-color wheel is made by chemist Michel Eugène Chevreul (1786–1889). Yellow, red, and blue again, with wrong complements and wrong afterimages. Yellow is not opposite purple, ultramarine blue is not opposite orange, and red is not the complement of green. His complements in "Simultaneous Contrast of Color," as he termed it, made mud. He never completed his solid model, and he was unable to discover a law of color harmony.

**1858** Verguin discovers magenta (fuchsine), the second basic dye that, at the time, superseded the use of mauve.

**1859** England—Physicist James Clerck Maxwell (1831–1879) publishes his "Theory of Color Vision," which is seen as the origin of colorimetry (quantitative color measurement).

**1859** Italy—Magenta is the new name of a rich pink-purple color derived from the bloody location of a battle in Italy—even though magenta is not blood red. It was transparent, but fugitive. Also called solferino.

**1860** Germany—Cobalt violet is developed (cobaltous crystalline phosphate, calcined cobalt oxide, and phosphorus oxide). A cool magenta color, it is required to make colors that fall between magenta and cyan, including ultramarine blue and azure (no other element can make this color). It sometimes contains arsenic and darkens (cobaltous oxide arsenate).

**1862** Japan—Japanese color wheel is recognized, with five colors: white, yellow, red, ultramarine blue, and black under a new color theory. Yellow came from white and blue from black, with no magenta or cyan. The internal prism spectrum is similar.

**1868** Germany—New colors are introduced: manganese violet, (manganese chloride, phosphoric acid, and ammonium carbonate), a permanent cool magenta.

**1868** England—Architect William Benson proposes and publishes his cuboid system, the first of his many color cubes.

**1870** New opaque, permanent colors are discovered, including cerulean blue (cobaltous stannate, made from cobalt oxide and tin oxide).

**1874** Germany—Wilhelm von Bezold (1837–1907) introduces his color cone, based on red, green, and blue as primaries.

**1874** Germany—Wilhelm Wundt (1832–1920), psychologist and philosopher, introduces his color sphere, which has eight basic colors: white and black are placed at the poles, and the equator comprises eight colors, including green, green-blue, blue, violet, purple, red, yellow, and yellow-green. The colors form a circle with gray at its center.

**1878** Austria—Physiologist Ewald Hering (1834–1918) theorizes three opposing sets of colors: yellow and ultramarine blue, red and green, and black and white. A different concept in its time, this opposed the purely phenomenal or physical understanding of colors

**1879** United States—American Nicholas Odgen Rood (1831–1902) makes a double cone color model, his "scientific" color circle, which he had constructed on the basis of experiments using rotating discs, a color point being placed precisely opposite its complementary partner. It had white on top and black at the bottom, and red, green, and blue as the triad. Although the development was a major contribution to color, magenta and cyan were still absent.

**1881** France—French Artist Seurat (1859–1891) touts "pointillism," the new scientific method, which includes the folly that red is the opposite of green. Although they do vibrate, there is no harmony.

**1886** Germany—The first and at the same time the last standard of pigment colors for artists is presented by A. W. Keim, of The German Society for the Promotion of Rational Methods in Painting. The following colors were deemed necessary by selected artists to set up control for the pigments in colors in an attempt to guarantee the color's characteristics and ingredients:

1. White lead
2. Zinc white
3. Cadmium yellow light and medium, and cadmium orange
4. Indian yellow
5. Naples yellow light and dark
6. Yellow to brown, natural and burnt ocher and sienna
7. Red ocher
8. Iron oxide colors
9. Graphite
10. Alizarin crimson madder lake (a magenta-colored fugitive pigment)
11. Vermilion
12. Umbers
13. Cobalt blue, native and synthetic
14. Ultramarine blue, natural and synthetic
15. Paris-Prussian blue
16. Oxide of chromium, opaque and transparent viridian
17. Green earth
18. Ivory black
19. Vine black

**1890** Thomas Young and Von Heimholtz develop the wave theory of light.

**1905** United States—American painter Albert Henry Munsell (1858–1918) creates an "eight-color wheel." His wheel was absent cyan, and his color opposites were incorrect. He darkened the colors with black, mixed them with gray, and tinted them with white, and numbered them all. This is still taught today.

**1909** Cadmium red is discovered.

**1915** United States—In his *Color Atlas,* Munsell introduces an order of colors—also known as a "color tree" due to its irregular outer profile grouped around a central vertical gray-scale. Munsell constructed his system around a circle with ten segments, arranging its colors at equal distances and selecting them in such a way that opposing pairs would result in an achromatic mixture.

**1916** Germany—Wilhelm Ostwald (1853–1932), the Nobel Prize winner for chemistry, compiles his Color Primer. His color circle was actually two cones that met at the flat circumferences of the top circles. The last color wheel (square) of college record was by Church-Ostwald. It has yellow, red, sea green, and ultramarine blue at the corners.

**1923** United States—Introduction of the first color-matching cabinets in which a sample could be matched under a variety of light sources. Prior to this, only daylight, which is very inconsistent, was used to match colors.

**1950** United States—ROYGBIV (red, orange, yellow, green, blue, indigo, and violet) is the "seven-color wheel." It is out of order and dispels the unity of opposition—more evidence that the color wheel has been misunderstood by every generation since, in and out of college.

**1990** United States—A new "color theory" is created by Color Your Carpet, Inc. for on-site re-dyeing of textiles, specifically carpets and rugs. The theory is applied to the system's proprietary dyeing process. Much like electronically produced colors, the spectrum is capable of millions of colors. Since carpet fibers (those that are re-dye-able) are actually transparent, and dyes are water-based and therefore transparent as well, the dyes that are in place from the factory can be re-dyed by introducing specially formulated dyes that "bond" with the existing dyes to become a "new color." This was the first true introduction of cyan, magenta, and yellow (not red, yellow, and blue) as the true primaries and the true basis of all colors in transparent color theory.

**1992** United States—A new "color wheel" is produced by the Color Wheel Company that is based on CYMK (cyan, yellow, magenta, and black), using thin film plastic and half-tone dpi (dots per square inch) colors. This color wheel is sold to printing, graphics, and textile companies. However, it is very limited in practical use, since only 40,000 colors are possible to display, and in the industries, (as on a computer today), more than 16 million colors are possible (depending on the number of available dye sites) in true transparent color when dyes are the coloring medium.

**1995** United States—Daniel Smith prints a "Color Square" using the "LAB" color chart. With white and black being the poles, this system is for not the artists who need to work with true opposition; it's better suited for the photo and printing industries. This model has the opposition colors, yellow and blue, on the top and bottom. Magenta and green are at the sides. A plus-and-minus number system relates the square with these colors as the primaries.

**1996** United States—A brilliant new color wheel called the Real Color Wheel is created by Don Jusko. This new theory more truly represents transparent colors and their relationship to each other.

There are 12 to 36 base colors in the Real Color Wheel, which joins the pigment and the light color wheel together as one, and agrees with the nature of your eyes' afterimage.

The main issues with current color wheels, except the Real Color Wheel, which is not yet available to the public, are the lack of defined differences of the following:

1.  Opaque colors (paint/pigments—solid mediums)
2.  Transparent colors (dyes—liquid mediums)
3.  Light colors (sunlight or electronic reproduction of light)

**2003** Artist Donald Jusko developed the Real Color Wheel—the only transparent 3 primary color wheel consisting of 36 rings of pigment with 360 hues. It is the only color wheel of its kind using color complements for mixing shadows and shade without the use of black pigment.

**2007** Congress passes a bill to ban incandescent bulbs by the year 2014. This change and elimination of the "warm" colored light will none-the-less impact the way we design spaces and specify color in the future.

**2009** Intelligent Color Engine technology and ICEmaker software reproaches the traditional RGB to CMYK color conversion challenge during printing to achieve "stable and vibrant color, and separate color automatically." FineEye Color approach recalculates color conversions that now accounts for paper color values during printing processes.

# interactive color websites

The following websites offer free interactive color tools that allow you to experiment with mixing primary and secondary hues; change and apply color to preset interior spaces, including bathrooms, bedrooms, dining rooms, living rooms, and kitchens; and develop different types of color harmonies, including monochromatic, contrast, triad, tetrad, and analogous. Also listed is a site where you can create and examine variations of Itten's seven color contrasts, as well as a site that allows you to explore meanings and associations between color and words.

1.  Online Color Mixing Palette for Painters
    http://painting.about.com/library/blpaint/blcolormixingpalette1.htm

2.  Sherwin-William's Color Visualizer
    http://www.sherwin.com/visualizer/

3.  Color Scheme Generator
    http://www.wellstyled.com/tools/colorscheme2/index-en.html

4.  Palette Picker
    http://www.worqx.com/color/palette.htm

5.  Cymbolism
    http://www.cymbolism.com

6.  Munsell Hue Test
    http://www.spectralcolor.com/game/huetest_kiosk

# glossary

**achromatic:** refers to black, white, and gray, each of which is without color.

**additive color:** color creation with light vs. pigment by *adding* the primary colors of light red, blue, and green in various combinations and intensities. Adding all colored light produces white light.

**alternation:** occurs when two design elements are repeated in sequence similar to repetition; however, the difference is the pattern includes two distinctly different elements (round to square, red to blue) versus one element repeating.

**analogous:** color schemes resulting from two or more colors adjacent to one another on the color wheel such as blue, blue-green, and green.

**anomaly:** an irregular deviation or departure from what one considers being normal. In interior design, this takes the form of contrasting two distinct styles where one becomes the focal point.

**anthropometrics:** the study of the average human body dimensions and measurements.

**asymmetry:** results when elements on either side of an implied axis are equal weight but vary in shape and size.

**balance:** refers to the relationship of colored elements as they occupy an implied axis within a space perceived to be equal in visual weight.

**Bezold effect:** Developed by rug maker Wilhelm von Bezold during the nineteenth century, the effect occurs when the largest color area is replaced by a new color creating a color interaction that changes the overall impression of the design.

**bari:** a package of garments to be worn sent by the groom's family to the bride, neatly wrapped and displayed a week before the wedding day.

**bio-inspired design:** Design that emulates the growth patterns, structures, and characteristics of natural occurring organisms (e.g., plants, animals, marine life).

**chroma:** refers to the purity of a color, completely absent of any white, gray, or black that would lessen its *intensity* or *saturation*, two additional terms acceptable for describing the color strength.

**chromatic colors:** any hue other than white, gray, and black.

**chromo therapy:** practice of using colored light and color in the environment to cure specific illness and in general to bring about beneficial healthy effects.

**color blindness:** a deficiency of color perception resulting in the inability to distinguish one or more colors.

**color continuation:** placement of one or more colors throughout an interior to create a continuous movement of the eye through the space.

**color grammar:** spatial relationship between various color arrangements and alignments to explore new design language.

**color interaction:** illusion that occurs when two or more hues interact placed next to one another changes our visual perception of the colors.

**color masking:** using color to hide design features through shading, color patterns, or blending to de-emphasize its presence within the space.

**Color Marketing Group:** a nonprofit organization that identifies global color trends in the marketplace.

**color rendering index (CRI):** indicates the light source's ability to render the true color of an object as it would appear in natural light using Kelvin to identify the color temperature.

# glossary

**complementary:** colors result from two colors opposite one another on the color wheel: red/green, blue/orange, and violet/yellow.

**cones:** the portion of cells within the retina of the eye responsible for seeing in day-light and recognizing color.

**contrast:** opposition in order to show or emphasize differences between two objects; the—juxtaposition of different forms, lines, or colors in a space to intensify each element's properties to produce a more dynamic experience, especially if it is unusual, is often the feature that earns the most attention.

**damask:** in paint and wallcovering, a pattern resulting from printing one color in matte and satin finish or light and darker values; in textiles, a reversible pattern made in cloth originated in Damascus during medieval times.

**Day of the Dead:** celebration in Mexico held yearly in October honoring those who have passed.

**diffraction:** the bending of light around objects producing light, dark, and/or different colored bands of light.

**direct color:** the manner of interfacing directly with a particular color source without obstruction.

**discord:** a loosely organized, disharmonized color combination that departs from the natural ordering of color.

**double complementary:** includes two adjacent hues and their complements on the color wheel such as yellow-green, green, red-violet, and red.

**emphasis:** a tool for creating points of interests not only for aesthetic purpose, but to orient users of the space.

**faux finish:** a painting or printing technique used to generate realistic three-dimensional objects including plants, wood, stone, marble, and other naturally occurring materials in two dimensions.

**Fibonacci Sequence:** a sequence of numbers where each successive number is the sum of the two previous numbers (e.g. 1, 1, 2, 3, 5, 8, 13, 21, 34, 55, 89, 144, etc.).

**focal point:** a *single* design element receiving the greatest visual emphasis in a room.

**fusuma:** traditional Japanese opaque sliding doors or shoji panels made of wood and paper used to screen rooms for privacy.

**Froebel blocks:** a series of wooden stacking blocks in various geometric shapes developed by German Frederick Froebel who created the concept of kindergarten in the 19th century.

**golden section:** also known as the golden rule, the rectangle, and the golden ratio, developed by the ancient Greeks, is the division of a line in two sections, where the ratio between the smallest section and the largest section is identical to the ratio between the largest section and the entire length of the line: $a$ is to $b$ as $b$ is to $a+b$ or ($a/b = b/a+b$).

**glossy/gloss:** a high sheen on a material surface usually reducing the intensity of the color.

**harmony:** the result of a perfect balance between individual color relationships.

**hue:** color that is the property of light by which the color of an object is classified and named as red, blue, green, or yellow in reference to the visible spectrum.

**indirect color:** natural or artificial light bouncing color from one colored surface onto adjoining surfaces where the original color becomes lighter in intensity.

**kalamandi:** images common in Baluch rugs are large hexagons filled with stylized patterns including trees.

**Kelvin:** the unit of measurement for color temperature of various light sources.

**Le Modular:** a measuring system developed by architect Le Corbusier based on the proportions of man.

**light reflectance value (LRV):** refers to the percentage of light that is reflected from a colored surface back into the interior space referenced in a range from 0–100.

**line:** the connection between two points in space.

**matte:** a dull, non-reflective surface. This surface texture typically makes colors appear darker.

# glossary

**Mayoun:** one of two festivals held during a traditional Pakistani wedding that celebrates the bride.

**Mehendi:** one of two festivals held during a traditional Pakistani wedding that celebrates the groom.

**metamerism:** the change is perception of a color influenced under different lighting conditions such as natural daylight in contrast to interior artificial light.

**memo:** a large textile sample that shows the full horizontal and vertical pattern repeats and color range of the design.

**monochromatic:** color scheme based on variations in value and chroma of one particular hue.

**multi-hue:** a color scheme that is not limited by the number hues but requires careful proportions to work effectively.

**nanometer:** the unit of measurement for different colored wavelengths within the visible spectrum.

**palette:** a range of colors assigned to the design for a particular interior space.

**primary hues:** red, yellow, and blue for pigment mixing; red, yellow and green for light mixing; cyan, magenta, and yellow for printing.

**programming:** the stage in the design process where you begin the data collection for a project.

**progression:** involves the repetition of similar elements with a continuous change (large to small, low to high, narrow to wide, light to dark).

**proportion:** the size relationships between elements (parts) and the visual composition or space (whole).

**pure hue:** is a color void of any white, gray, or black and is at its highest intensity or brightness. These colors are the product of mixing various amounts of primary and secondary colors.

**radiation:** concentric color arrangement instead of objects to unify design elements and create visual movement versus the traditional sense where it is an arrangement of objects in a radial pattern.

**radial:** balance that is achieved by the equal rotation of design elements around a central axis.

**reflection:** the bouncing of one or more colored wavelengths of light off an object resulting in the color of the object seen.

**refraction:** the bending of light resulting from being slowed as it moves from one medium through a denser medium.

**repetition:** the systematic orderly succession of identical design elements (shape, line, color, form) along a define path in space.

**rods:** the portion of cells within the retina of the eye responsible for seeing in dim light and recognizing values.

**Saltillo:** a porous, non-glazed, clay tile handmade in the Mexican city of Saltillo commonly made in reds, oranges, and yellows.

**satin finish:** a material with a medium sheen reflecting less light than a gloss but more than a matte surface.

**scale:** refers to the size of a shape in relation to a given known, in most cases, the human body and its position within space.

**secondary hues:** violet, green, and orange each made from combining two primary hues.

**shade:** physically or visually adding varying amounts of black to any pure hue reducing the color's intensity.

**shalwar kameez:** or loose pajama-like clothing to be worn by the bride during the Mayoun festival; one of two festivals celebrated the week before a traditional Pakistani wedding.

**shape:** one or more line connecting to form a two-dimensional image such as a square, circle, or triangle.

**sherwani:** the traditional white, long coat-like coat garment embroidered in gold worn by men during the traditional Pakistani wedding.

**simultaneous contrast:** when any two colors are place side by side or surrounded by one or the other resulting in a change is the colors' visual perception. This effect is intensified with complementary colors of high saturation or brightness and dramatic.

**Spanish colonial:** a mélange of styles with open courtyards, tiled roofs, archways, heavy wooden doors, and plain stucco wall surfaces.

**split complementary:** color scheme composed of three colors consisting of one main hue plus the two hues each adjacent to its complement (for example, blue, red-orange, and yellow-orange).

**subtractive color:** pigment color mixing using paint, dyes, colorants, and inks where red, blue, and yellow are commonly identified as the primary colors. The *subtraction* of all color produces white.

**symmetry:** the arrangement of elements on either side of an implied axis that are equally balanced and of the same shape and form (i.e., *mirror image*).

**tetrad:** color schemes composed of four colors equally spaced along the color wheel such as yellow, red-orange, violet, and blue-green.

**tertiary hues:** red-violet, blue-violet, blue-green, yellow-green, yellow-orange, and red-orange, each made by combining a secondary hue with one of the primaries.

**texture:** the characteristic visual and tactile quality of the surface of a material resulting from the way in which the materials are constructed or combined together.

**tint:** physically or visually adding varying amounts of white to any pure hue reducing the color's intensity.

**tone:** physically or visually adding varying amounts of gray to any pure hue reducing the color's intensity.

**triad/triadic:** color schemes composed of three colors equally spaced along the color wheel such as green, purple, and orange.

**uniform connectedness:** occurs when design elements are connected by uniform visual properties, such as color, will be perceived as more related than design elements that are not connected by some visual design tool.

**unity:** the repetition of color to achieve a unified whole.

**value:** refers to the lightness or darkness of a color.

**variety:** the combination of one or more color elements with shape, form, pattern, and texture to create diversity and contrast in an interior space.

**vibrancy:** the perception of movement at the boundary between two highly saturated colors often recognized with complements.

**visible spectrum:** the portion of colored light within the electromagnetic spectrum visible to the human eye.

**wayfinding:** text, symbols and color cue techniques used to orient and assist in physical awareness of one's place or orientation in space.

# bibliography

Albers, Josef. (1975). *Interaction of color.* London: Yale University Press.

American Marketing Association. (July/August 2005). Coloring Your World. *Marketing Management,* p. 5.

Arnheim, Rudolf. (1969). *Visual thinking.* Berkeley: University of California Press.

_____. (1974). *Art and visual perception.* Berkeley: University of California Press.

_____. (1972). *Art and visual perception: A psychology of the creative eye.* Berkeley: University of California Press.

Ball, Victoria K. (1965). The aesthetics of color: A review of fifty years of experimentation. *The Journal of Aesthetics and Art Criticism,* 23(4), 441–452.

Benz, Ernest, Izutsu, Toshihiko, Portman, Adolf, et al. (1972). *Color symbolism.* Dallas: Spring Publications.

Bernard, Teresa. (n.d.). *Art Lesson: Principles of Good Design—Contrast.* Retrieved September 18, 2008, from http://www.bluemoonwebdesign.com/art-lessons-4.asp

Binggeli, Corky. (2007). *Interior Design A Survey.* Hoboken, NJ: John Wiley & Sons.

Birren, Faber. (1969). *Principles of color: A review of past traditions and modern theories of color harmony.* New York: Van Nostrand Reinhold.

_____. (1992). *The power of color: How it can reduce fatigue, relieve monotony, enhance sexuality, and more.* Secaucus, NJ: Citadel Press.

_____. (1969). *Principles of color.* New York: Van Nostrand Reinhold Company.

Brainard, Shirl. (2003). *A Design Manual* (3rd ed.). New Jersey: Prentice Hall.

Brusatin, Manlio. (1991). *A history of color.* Boston: Shambhala Publications.

Burchett, Kenneth E. (2005). *A bibliographical history of the study and use of color from aristotle to kandinsky.* New York: Edwin Mellen Press.

Ching, Francis D.K. (1996). *Architecture: Form, Space, & Order* (2nd ed.). New York: John Wiley & Sons, Inc.

Ching, Francis D.K., & Binggeli, Corky. (2005). *Interior design illustrated.* Hoboken, NJ: John Wiley & Sons.

Cohan, Tony, Takahashi, Masako, & Levick, Melba. (1998). *Mexicolor: The spirit of Mexican design.* San Francisco: Chronicle Books.

Color Marketing Group. (2008). *The Profit of Color.* Retrieved September 14, 2008, from http://www.colormarketing.org/uploadedFiles/Media/The%20Profit%20of%20Color!%20-%20FINAL%204%2007.pdf?TierSlicer51_TSMenuTargetID=650&TierSlicer51_TSMenuTargetType=2&TierSlicer51_TSMenuID=51

Color Matters. (2008). *Drunk Tank Pink.* Retrieved February 16, 2009, from http://www.colormatters.com/body_pink.html

COLOURlovers. (2007). *11 Great Color Legends.* Retrieved on May 27, 2008, from http://www.colourlovers.com/blog/2007/05/01/11-great-color-legends/print/

Commission for Architecture and the Built Environment. (2008). *The Richard Desmond Children's Eye Centre.* Retrieved September 18, 2008, from http://www.betterpublicbuilding.org.uk/finalists/2007/desmond/

Cranz, Galen (2000). *The Chair: Rethinking Culture, Body, and Design.* New York: W.W. Norton & Company.

Daggett, Dr. Williard R., Cobble, Jeffrey E., & Gertel, Steven J. (2008). *Color in an optimum learning environments.* Retrieved November 11, 2008, from http://www.sagusinternational.com/downloads/resource_dtails.asp?ID=3&s=6&s2=6&p=6

# bibliography

Department of Homeland Security. *Homeland security advisory system*. Retrieved September 11, 2008, from http://www.dhs.gov/xabout/laws/gc_1214508631313.shtm

D'Imperio, Connie B. (2007). History of Color Systems. Retrieved November 12, 2008 from http://www.coloryourcarpet.com

Droste, Magdalena. (2006). Bauhaus 1919–1933. Los Angeles, CA: Taschen.

Dubé, Richard L. (1997). *A pattern language: A practical source for landscape design*. New York: Van Nostrand Reinhold.

Edmunds Inc. (2008). *Traffic Ticket Urban Legends: Debunking 10 Driving Myths that all Your Friends Believe*. Retrieved on November 12, 2008, from http://www.edmunds.com/advice/youngdrivers/articles/125550/article.html

Edwards, Betty. (2004). *Color: A course in mastering the art of mixing colors*. New York: Tarcher/Penguin Books.

Eiseman, Leatrice. (1998). *Color for your every mood*. Sterling, VA: Capital Books.

_____. (2006). *Color: Messages and meaning*. Massachusetts: Hand Books Press.

Elam, Kimberly. (2001). *Geometry in design: Studies in proportion and composition*. New York: Princeton Architectural Press.

Ellinger, Richard G. (1980). *Color structure and design*. New York: Van Nostrand Reinhold.

Faimon, Peg, & Weigand, John. (2004). *The nature of design*. Cincinnati: How Design Books.

Fehrman, Kenneth & Cherie. (2004). *Color: The secret influence*. Upper Saddle River: NJ: Pearson Education.

Feisner, Edith Anderson. (2006). *Color Studies* (2nd ed.). New York: Fairchild Publications Inc.

Feldman, Edmund Burke. (1992). *Varieties of visual experience* (4th ed.). Upper Saddle River, NJ: Prentice Hall.

Flags of the World. *Italy*; retrieved September 13, 2008, from: http://flagspot.net/flags/it.html

Ford, Janet Lynn. (n.d.). *Worqx*. Retrieved September 7, 2008, from www.worqx.com/color/color_proportion.htm

Frederick, Mathew. (2007). *101 Things I learned in architecture school*. Cambridge, MA: MIT Press.

Froebel Web. (2002). *Johannes Itten 1888–1967*. Retrieved on September, 5, 2008, from http://www.froebelweb.org/web2018.html

Gage, John. (1993). *Color and Culture: Practice and Meaning from Antiquity to Abstraction*. Berkley, CA: University of California Press.

Gibbs, Jenny. (2005). *Interior design: A practical guide*. New York: Harry N. Abrams, Inc.

Goldberg, Paul, & Becom, Jeffery. (2003). *Mediterranean color*. New York: Abbeville Press.

Hardy, Paula. (2007). *Lonely Planet Morocco* (7th ed.). Oakland, CA: Lonely Planet Publications.

Holtzschue, Linda. (2006). *Understanding color: An introduction for designers*. Hoboken, NJ: John Wiley & Sons.

Hope, Augustine, & Walch, Margaret. (1990). *The color compendium*. New York: Van Nostrand Reinhold.

Itten, Josef. (2001). *The elements of color*. Hoboken, NJ: John Wiley & Sons.

Khouw, Natalie. (2007). *The Meaning of Color for Gender*. Retrieved June 22, 2009, from http://www.colormatters.com/khouw.html

Knight, Terry W. (1998). Color grammars: The representation of form and color in designs. *Leonardo*, 26(2), 117–124.

Kobayashi, Shigenobu. (1987). *A book of colors*. Tokyo: Kodansha International.

_____. (1990). *Color image scale*. Tokyo: Kodansha International.

Koenig, Becky. (2007). *Color workbook* (2nd ed.). Upper Saddle River, NJ: Pearson Education.

Kopacz, Jeanne. (2004). *Color in three-dimensional design*. New York: McGraw-Hill.

Kopec, David. *The importance of color in home sales*. Retrieved March 17, 2006, from http://realtytimes.com/rtapages/20030513_color.htm

Lauer, David A., & Pentak, Stephen. (2007). Basic design (6th ed.). Belmont, CA: Wadsworth/Thomas Learning.

Lehndorff, Betsy. (2002, October 5). Living color. *Rocky Mountain News*, p. 1E.

# bibliography

Leland, Nita. (1998). *Exploring color: How to use and control color in your painting.* Cincinnati: North Light Books.

Lidwell, William, Holden, Kristina, & Butler, Jill. (2003). *Universal principles of design.* Beverly, MA: Rockport Publishers.

Machin, Rob. (2005). *Trigger Happy.* Retrieved on June 23, 2009, from http://emea.promax.tv/emea/dec_news_1.html

Mahnke, Frank H. (1996). *Color, environment, and human response.* New York: John Wiley & Sons.

Mahnke, Frank H., & Rudolf H. (1987). *Color and light in man-made environments.* New York: Van Nostrand Reinhold Company.

Malnar, Joy Monice, & Vodvarka, Frank. (1992). *The interior dimension: a theoretical approach to enclosed space.* New York: John Wiley & Sons.

Marshall Editions Limited. (1980). *Color.* Los Angeles: Knapp Press.

McCleary, Kathleen. (2002, September 29). Living Colors. *USA Weekend,* p. 5.

McNeil, Patrick. (2007). *The design principle: Emphasis.* Retrieved September 15, 2008, from http://www.designmeltdown.com/chapters/Emphasis/

Meerwein, Gerhard, Rodeck, Bettina, & Mahnke, Frank H. (2007). *Color: Communication in architectural space.* Base, Switzerland: Birkhäuser Verlag AG.

Morton, Jill. (1997). *A guide to color symbolism.* [Electronic version] Honolulu: Colorcom.

_____. (2008). *Color Matters for the Home.* [Electronic version]. Honolulu: Colorcom.

_____. (2004). *Global color clues and taboos.* [Electronic version]. Honolulu: Colorcom. New York: McGraw-Hill.

Munsell, Albert. (1905). *A Color Notation.* Boston, MA: Geo. H. Ellis Co.

Nielson, Karla J., & Taylor, David A. (2007). *Interiors: An Introduction* (4th ed.). New York: McGraw-Hill.

Ormiston, Rosalind, & Robinson, Michael. (2007). *Colour source book.* London: Flame Tree Publishing.

Pile, John. (1997). *Color in interior design.* New York: McGraw-Hill.

Rengel, Roberto. (2007). *Shaping Interior Space* (2nd ed.). New York: Fairchild Publishers.

Robertson, A. R. Computation of correlated color temperature and distribution temperature. *Journal of the Optical Society of America,* 58, 1528–1968.

Rompilla, Ethel. (2005). *Color for interior design.* New York: Harry N. Abrams.

Routio, Pentti. (2004, March 31). *Theory of Design.* Retrieved January 18, 2006, from http://membres.lycos.fr/routio/122.htm

Singh, Satyendra. (2006). Impact of Color on Marketing. *Journal of Management Decision,* 44(6), 783–789.

Skorinko, Jeanin L., Kemmer, Suzanne, Hebel, Michelle R., & Lane, David M. (2006). A Rose by Any Other Name . . . : Color-Naming Influences on Decision Making. *Psychology & Marketing,* 23(12), 975–993.

Slotkis, Susan J. (2006). *Foundations of interior design.* New York: Fairchild Publications.

Smith, Dianne. (2008). Color-person-environment relationships. *Color Research and Application,* 33(4) 312–319.

Stewart, Mary. (2002). *Launching the imagination: A comprehensive guide to basic design.* New York: McGraw-Hill

Stimpson, Miriam. (1987). *Modern Furniture Classics.* New York: Watson-Guptill Publications.

Stone, Nancy J., & English, Anthony J. (1998). Task Type, Posters, and Workspace Color on Mood, Satisfaction, and Performance. *Journal of Environmental Psychology 18(2),* 175–185.

Tazawa, Yutaka. (1973). *Japan's cultural history: A perspective.* Japan: Ministry of Foreign Affairs.

Uribes, Johanna. (2008). *Color—Does it Really Affect Your Mood?* Retrieved on November 12, 2008, from http://www.johannauribes.com/freearticle1.php

Versa. (n.d.). *Color symbolism by culture.* Retrieved September 11, 2008, from http://www.versacreative.com/au/vault/inside_design/colour_symbolism.htm

Wong, Wucius. (1997). *Principles of color design.* New York: John Wiley & Sons.

Xerox. (2008). International Color Guide—Mexico, Mexico's Color Palette Is a Mix of Historical Associations and the Environment's Deeply Toned Offerings. Retrieved on September 15, 2008, from http://www.office.xerox.com/small-business/tips/color-guide/mexico/enus.html

Yoshino Japanese Antiques. (n.d.). *Elements of a traditional Japanese interior.* The Yoshino Newsletter. Retrieved September 15, 2008, from http://www.yoshinoantiques.com/Interior-article.html

Zelanski, Paul, & Fisher, Mary Pat. (1995). *Shaping space: The dynamics of three-dimensional design.* Belmont, CA: Wadsworth/Thomas Learning Publishing.

_____. (1999). *Color.* Upper Saddle River, NJ: Prentice Hall.

# credits

# index

# index